PRIORITIES
AND
PEOPLE

PRIORITIES AND PEOPLE

BY
HARRY BAKER ADAMS

THE BETHANY PRESS
St. Louis, Missouri

Library of Congress Cataloging in Publication Data

Adams, Harry Baker, 1924-
  Priorities and people.

  Includes bibliographical references.
  1. Christian life—1960-   2. Decision-
making (Ethics) I. Title.
BV4501.2.A28   248'.4   75-31692
ISBN 0-8272-2924-0

Cover art by DeVere Shoop

One of the scribes . . . asked him,
"Which commandment is the first of all?"

Jesus answered, "The first is,

Hear, O Israel:
The Lord our God, the Lord is one;
and you shall love the Lord your God
with all your heart,
and with all your soul,
and with all your mind,
and with all your strength.

"The second is this,

You shall love your neighbor as yourself.

"There is no other commandment greater than these."
—Mark 12:28-31.

Contents

Preface

Recently we have been made acutely conscious of the fact that the resources of this earth are limited. No doubt we have known this all along, but for at least a generation we in the western world have been living as though the resources available to us were infinitely expendable. Suddenly we are faced with an energy crisis and the grim specter of world hunger. With famine taking its toll of millions of lives, we are vividly aware that the world's food supply is limited. As the human population grows with alarming rapidity, concern for the quality of life on this planet continues to mount.

The fundamental conditions of human existence force us to think about priorities. Because we are finite beings with a limited life span, priorities are expressed in every action we take and in every decision we make. What is true on a world scale may be seen more clearly, perhaps, as we reflect on the situations of individual persons.

For persons with sharply limited incomes, which includes most of us, the purchase of a television set signifies that owning a TV is more important than doing something else with our money. Even the affluent do not have unlimited resources for meeting all of the urgent requests of those who plead for help. Our priorities tend to shape the ways we use our resources and spend our money. Or to view the situation in a different perspective, how we use our resources and spend our money reflect the actual priorities we set for our lives.

Money is not our only limited resource. We have only so much energy to expend, and we expend it in doing those things we regard as most important. We have only so much time granted to us, and we use it according to the priorities which we set for ourselves. We can give serious attention to only a limited number of concerns, and where we direct our attention indicates what we consider to be of greatest significance.

Institutions and societies, as well as individuals, set priorities and shape their lives according to the ranking they give to values and goals. For example, a college faces a choice of building a new dormitory or a new laboratory. Its decision will reflect a judgment as to whether living conditions on campus or educational resources are more important. A church has to decide whether to give major support to the education of its ministry or to an inner city project, or to give limited support to both. A society confronts decisions as to how it will use its resources: how much it will spend for armaments and defense, for medical care, for human welfare, for public housing, for transportation. Actual decisions will reflect priorities in a society's values.

The decisions which individuals and human institutions make in regard to the use of their resources, energy, time, and attention are determined on the basis of a set of priorities. How does a person or an institution determine priorities? How do we decide what things are really of first importance? The answer to such questions is usually rather complex.

Priorities may be consciously set when a person deliberates on his options and decides that one possible course is more significant than another. This choice reflects a judgment that the goals of a particular course are more worthy or that the values to be achieved are more meaningful. But what makes goals worthy or values meaningful? Here we touch on fundamental commitments of human existence. On the basis of our experience and reflection we make commitments to goals and values which we deem to be truly significant and worth the investment of our lives.

Or priorities may be consciously set when we find ourselves obligated to be obedient to some principle or law or rule. For example, we are confronted by the commandment: "You shall not bear false witness against your neighbor." Consequently, telling the truth has priority over any gain we might realize by speaking falsely about another. The law establishes 55 miles an hour as the speed limit on the highway and decrees certain penalties for persons caught violating this law. Respect for the law and fear of the consequences of violating it persuade us that holding our speed to 55 miles an hour is more important than the time gained by driving 70 miles an hour.

③ Some priorities by which we live may be simply accepted with little or no conscious reflection. Certain things seem important to us because they are given primacy in the culture and society in which we live. It's just the way things are; we take our personal priorities from the community which sustains and shapes our lives. Also, there are some priorities which reflect our personal or psychological needs. Our need for security or approval may take precedence so that we evaluate what we say and the decisions we make in terms of how they are going to meet these needs.

These observations about how priorities are set indicate some of the complexities involved when we seek to determine what things are important to us. However, the process by which priorities are set is not our primary concern in this discussion. Our intent here is simply to recognize that persons, with some measure of freedom, can and do establish their priorities. We are assuming that persons bear responsibility for the priorities they set and for the decisions which result from their judgments about what things are of first importance.

Our discussion so far suggests that our priorities are related to and express the values we hold. We invest our resources, time, energies, and ourselves in relation to our assessment of the values involved. If we give more attention to a piece of property than we do to a person, this is a clear indication of the relative importance we assign to the two. If we as a nation invest more money in highways than in the arts, this decision reflects what we regard as of more value to society. As we reflect on the priorities set by our nation, our community, our congregation, or our neighbors, we need to be aware that we are dealing with fundamental values of life. We are dealing with basic decisions which persons make about the good, the true, and the worthy.

In the discussion which follows, it is our purpose to become aware of the values which we affirm in our relationships with one another and to explore how the priorities we set affect our dealings with persons as we seek to express our Christian commitment. Our basic thesis is that the first priority for a Christian focuses on how we treat one another as persons. In human relationships, a Christian seeks to affirm the worth of persons and to order his or her priorities to attain this goal.

Immediately, we are confronted by several perplexing questions. What does it mean to affirm persons and to seek the fulfillment of their personhood? How does our faith in and commitment to God as revealed in Jesus Christ inform the priorities we set? In our relationships with persons, what kind of decisions should we expect to issue from the priorities we set as Christians? What sources of strength does the Christian faith make available to us as we attempt to express the priorities we affirm as followers of Jesus Christ?

There are, of course, a number of ways we could talk about how to be faithful and responsible to our Christian commitment in our relationships with persons. For our discussion here we have chosen to explore how we may live responsibly as Christians in terms of the priorities we set for ourselves.

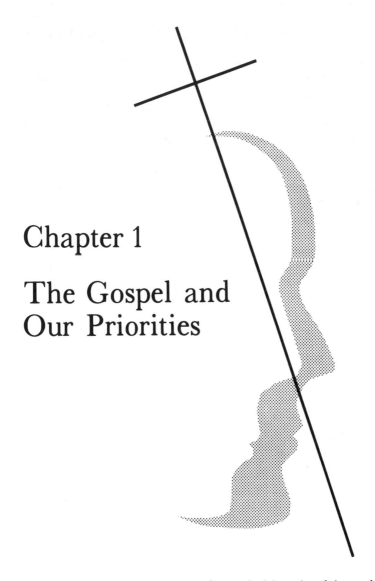

Chapter 1

The Gospel and Our Priorities

Two persons are facing significant decisions involving values and priorities. One is a medical researcher who needs to try out a new drug on human subjects. This drug has a potential for assisting in the treatment of cancer, but its effect on persons has never been tested. Until it is thoroughly tested, obviously there is a risk involved to those who take it. However, it cannot be tested until it is used with persons.

As the researcher ponders this dilemma, she weighs a number of values and lives out some priorities. How does she balance the potential future good to the whole society against the risk involved for the person who first takes the drug? In her eagerness to push on with her research, how honest can she be about the hazards involved with those who volunteer to use it? To what extent is she being motivated by a desire for the acclaim awaiting the person who succeeds in finding an effective drug? Is she sufficiently concerned that those who volunteer to take the drug are making a responsible decision?

In this situation the researcher must be asking herself if the research project, which has its own satisfactions, is beginning to outweigh her concern for the good which will be done for people. Clearly she is facing decisions which express the fundamental priorities of her life.

Another person facing a significant decision is a young man in his senior year of high school. As he approaches graduation he has to decide whether to accept admission to college or to take a job that has been offered to him. He too is weighing a number of values and living out some priorities. What will be the effect on his life of the time spent in furthering his education? How important are the wishes of his parents in this decision? Is there sufficient compensation in further education to warrant the postponement of things he could buy with the money he could earn if he started to work now?

This high school senior must weigh the advantages and disadvantages of a college education. Does it offer the prospect of earning far more money in the long run? If not, what other values would a college education afford? Like the medical researcher, this student is facing a decision which will express the fundamental priorities of his life.

Each one of us sets priorities for our lives. We judge some things to be more important than others. The actions we take and the decisions we make reflect our judgment as to what really counts in life. The setting of priorities for our lives is a universal experience in which all of us share.

If this is true, what is unique about a Christian's role in ordering his or her priorities? Surely, a Christian has no monopoly on insights into how persons should deal responsibly with one another. Nevertheless, the Christian faith does provide us an invaluable resource for determining what is of genuine importance both for our personal living and our relationships with others.

Just how the Christian faith is relevant to the ordering of our priorities is the issue we wish to explore.

Context for Our Decisions

As we seek to identify the values, goals, and purposes that are of major importance for our life in relationship with others, we find ourselves in a context which has been shaped by Christian affirmation and witness. In the broad context of the whole of Western culture, the Christian faith has had a profound influence. Our art, marriage customs, legal codes, architecture, literature, thought patterns, ethical norms, family arrangements—all these have been permeated by the influence of the Christian tradition.

The preceding statement is neither a claim that our Western culture can be defined as Christian nor an assertion that the Christian faith is the sole determinant of how we think or act. It is simply a recognition that the affirmations of the Christian faith have had significant impact on the whole pattern of life in which we find ourselves. Because we are influenced by the standards of our time and place, when we set priorities for our lives, the impact of the gospel on our culture shapes the values and goals which we deem to be important.

As we attempt to assess the impact of the gospel on our culture and on ourselves, perhaps we should make clear what is meant by the gospel. To state it simply and directly, the gospel is the good news that God loves us. Through Jesus Christ, God has come into our world not only to say that he loves us, but to express that love as he shares our lives with us. So we are talking about the impact on our world and on ourselves of the biblical affirmation that "God so loved the world that he gave his only Son, that whoever believes in him should not perish but have eternal life" (John 3:16).

This is what is meant when we say that the gospel, the good news of God's love revealed to us in Jesus Christ, has made an impact on our culture and shapes the values and goals which we deem to be important. Moreover, in a more restricted context, the gospel has made an impact on our determination of what is significant through the church.

The church, which carries the tradition of the Christian heritage, affirms the witness of the gospel in our present situation. As we become involved in the church, the gospel provides a context in which we order our goals and values. At least that is the role and function of the church as it is described in the New Testament.

We are aware, of course, that our experiences in the church do not always measure up to our expectations. The church today has many critics. Often it is charged with being more concerned about its self-preservation as an institution than about witnessing to the radical demands of the gospel. Some persons view it as a bastion of conservatism in which those who are comfortably situated isolate themselves from the poor, the oppressed, and the outcast. There is a widespread feeling that people within the church respond more to the pressures and demands of the world than they do to the claims of the gospel.

A study of an experiment in church renewal provides a sobering observation. It noted that when the church moved to pursue actions that were not considered respectable by the community and business leaders, those who were involved in the business community dropped out. "These people offered reasons other than their fear of reprisal," the report noted. "But the evidence of social science overwhelmingly attests that people seldom become actively involved and identified with activities threatening to their financial security."[1] Such studies lead many persons to feel that the church is irrelevant to the concerns of ordinary people and that the Sunday confessions of its members bear little resemblance to their Monday actions.

Honesty compels us to acknowledge that much of the criticism of the church is well-taken. After all, it is a human institution. Its members are the same persons who populate the Rotary Club, the labor union, the beauty parlor, the Chamber of Commerce, the democratic town committee, the fire department. But in spite of its obvious faults and failings, the church is still the church. Or, to put it another way, through its frail humanity the church is still the church.

---

[1]*Gideon's Gang* by Jeffrey K. Hadden and Charles F. Longino, Jr. Pilgrim Press, 1974, p. 55.

Somehow in his mysterious way, God is still at work in this community of faith which has never completely escaped the claim that it is the Body of Christ, the people of God, a holy nation. Of course, we have learned not to make exclusive claims for the church, for surely God is also at work in the world outside the church. But with appropriate reserve and necessary humility we dare to claim that the church does, in fact, carry the tradition of the Christian heritage and affirms the witness of the gospel.

The gospel as it is perceived by the church provides the context in which we set priorities for our lives. Our lives are nurtured, sometimes well and sometimes poorly to be sure, in a Christian community where the Scriptures are read regularly, where God is acknowledged as the Creator of the world and of our lives, where the redeeming power of Christ is announced and demonstrated, and where the love of God for sinners is manifest. At times the church's teaching may be less than adequate, its preaching less than inspiring, its business meetings less than edifying. Nevertheless, we are exposed to a community which has endured only by the grace of God, and something of God's grace has come into our lives.

It is in this context of the gospel, manifest in the church, that we try to figure out what is important as we find ourselves relating to other persons.

Directives of the Gospel

As we struggle with priorities in this context which the gospel helps to shape, does the gospel give any specific direction as to ways our relationships with other persons are to be ordered? Surely the answer is yes. For the gospel does speak to what the goods and values of life are and how they should be ranked. However, we need to explore in some detail what it means to say that the gospel gives direction for the setting of priorities for our lives.

Some of the ways in which the gospel directives for life have been perceived are inadequate and misleading. For example, the gospel may be understood as providing a set of rules which give us appropriate moral direction in any situation. These rules may be identified with the Ten Commandments, with our own summary of the "laws of God" derived from the Scriptures, or with a series of moral maxims distilled from the teachings of Jesus. However such a set of rules may be derived, the gospel is viewed as providing us with an authoritative set of principles which need only to be obeyed in order to fulfill our ethical obligations in all human relationships.

Also, the life and teachings of Jesus may be viewed as providing us with a blueprint for ordering the priorities of life. Jesus offers a pattern for ways in which these priorities get expressed in daily living. If we want to know what our priorities should be, we can simply look at the kind of priorities Jesus set for his life. If we want to know how to deal with a particular situation, we need only to find out how Jesus dealt with a comparable situation. According to this point of view, Jesus, as the complete person, serves as the model for us in ordering our lives. In situations requiring an ethical judgment, we may simply ask, "What would Jesus do?"

A third way in which gospel directives for life may be perceived is to focus on the experience of the earliest Christians. The New Testament describes how the early church did things and how the first Christians dealt with one another and with their neighbors in the world. Those first followers of Jesus, as well as Jesus himself, offer us a model for ordering our priorities. In the Acts of the Apostles and in Paul's letters to the churches, we may discern the needed directives for achieving right relationships in all of our dealings with others.

Appealing as these three ways of discerning the gospel's directives for life may be, nevertheless they are inadequate and misleading as a basis for setting our priorities. This judgment is made in light of our understanding of the gospel and the character of human experience.

The gospel, as we are interpreting it, is not a rigid set of rules about human behavior. Rather it is a testimony to and expression of the dynamic love of God for his people. The Bible offers us not so much a set of timeless, eternal principles, but rather an account of the activity of God in the midst of his world. Moreover, human existence is not an endless repetition of set patterns to be governed mechanically by eternal laws. Instead, persons find themselves repeatedly in new situations to which they must respond with creative insight and freedom.

In regard to our human situation, James Gustafson has pointed out, "there is no fixed timeless order of priority of the values of human life which *a priori* determines what ought to occur in all particular circumstances." Recognizing that "God's purposes for man might be summed up in some generalized unitary conception, such as 'He wills man's good,' " Professor Gustafson observes that "man's good is a complex and not simple notion."[2]

We need to affirm, however, that the gospel does give us direction as we set priorities for our lives and seek to express those priorities in our words and deeds. While the "law of God" as articulated in the Scriptures may not give an exhaustive guide to human behavior, it does set forth the fundamental realities of our human relationships. These realities must be taken seriously as we make decisions about what we are going to do in the particular, complex situations we face.

Consider, for example, the commandment, "You shall not kill." We recognize the moral imperative of this biblical injunction. But suppose we find ourselves in a position where we deem that the taking of the life of another is a forced necessity—for reasons of self-defense, to defend the lives of others, or because we are involved in a war which we regard as just. Certainly we would not take another's life without much anguished wrestling and reaching a firm conviction that it is the only way some larger good can be served. This commandment lays a firm claim on our lives, although we may not feel we can take it as a rigid absolute.

The life of Jesus may not offer a pattern which we can imitate in precise detail, yet the presence of Jesus Christ in our world certainly does inform us about the priorities which are appropriate for human existence. His ways of dealing with persons and situations shows us the values we need to seek as we face specific circumstances. The ways he related to persons illuminate our own situations as we act toward and with others. The goals to which he dedicated his life help us to articulate goals appropriate for our lives.

Many persons have an impact on us as we seek to shape our lives and struggle to understand what is required of us in our

---

[2]James Gustafson, *Christian Ethics and the Community.* Pilgrim Press, 1971, p. 144.

relationships with others. Parents, friends, sons and daughters, admired figures in public life, teachers, pastors, coaches, saints—all these exert an influence on us. Yet we may not feel it is needful or desirable to pattern our lives after any of them. For persons who are nutured in the Christian faith Jesus Christ performs this role supremely.

When we look at Jesus we see a person who has his priorities straight. In his life and teachings, as well as in his dealings with persons, we discern a human being who manifests the truth of God. Yet we do not hear him saying to us, "Be like me." Instead, we hear him saying, "Be the person whom God the Creator and God the Father intends you to be." Looking at Jesus we see a model, the kind of person, God intended for his human creatures.

In this same manner the experience of the first Christians and the early church speaks to us of what is appropriate for us today. Their experience offers no precise equivalent to ours in regard to the specific situations involved. However, in the ways they first came under the impact of Jesus Christ and dealt with the issues they faced, we may discern how the impact of Jesus Christ on our lives gets expressed in facing the issues that confront us.

We may recall, for example, the gifts of the Spirit which the apostle Paul so ably described in First Corinthians 12:7. Would we use this identical language to talk about the gifts of the Spirit in the church today? Yet Paul's discerning insight that "to each is given the manifestation of the Spirit for the common good" helps us as we deal with one another's gifts in our congregations.

Precisely, then, how does the gospel provide directives for setting our priorities and working out our relationships with others?

We have struggled to affirm that the gospel has a great deal to say to us in this regard. Yet we need to recognize that not even the gospel, especially *not* the gospel, takes away the need for employing our own sensitive and creative insights as we deal with our particular situations. It does not presume to offer us a set of rules to be followed slavishly or mechanically. The gospel is a gift from God to be used imaginatively as we bear the awesome responsibility of making decisions about our priorities and how we should deal with persons.

It is the function of the gospel to remind us of who we are as followers of Jesus Christ and to enable us to discern a style of life which reflects a Christian commitment.

Our First Priority

What kind of priorities does the gospel set for our lives? When we consider that every decision we make reflects the priorities we hold, what may we regard as priorities that are shaped significantly by the gospel? If we take seriously the directives of the gospel, what things should we deem as of first importance? Earlier we suggested that the first priority for a Christian focuses on how we treat one another as persons. We need to recognize, however, that the complexities lurking beneath this rather simple affirmation compel careful and sustained reflection if we are to grasp the manner in which the gospel gets expressed in our words and deeds. Nevertheless, this affirmation suggests a beginning point for launching our exploration.

In terms of a Christian understanding of who we are and how we are expected to live with one another, we suggest that what happens to persons ranks as our first priority. Persons have priority. As we seek to express in our lives what is right and good, this right and good is to be measured in terms of what happens to persons.

Our conviction that the worth of persons is the supreme value to be affirmed by Christians finds support in current ethical thought. Paul Lehmann talks repeatedly about "making and keeping human life human."[3] John Macquarrie asserts that "the Christian is faced with the more demanding task of trying to work out an ethic that allows for the fullest development of the individual within an equitable social framework."[4] What makes an ethic "right" or "appropriate" is the full development of the individual.

"Biblically speaking," argues William Stringfellow, "the singular, straightforward issue of ethics—and the elementary topic of politics—is *how to live humanly during the Fall.*"[5] Cries of protest are directed against those institutions or individual actions which dehumanize persons, whether it be in a prison or on an assembly line. Whatever dehumanizes persons is evil; whatever makes personal existence more human is good.

---

[3]Paul Lehmann, *Ethics in a Christian Context.* Harper & Row, 1963.
[4]John Macquarrie, *Three Issues in Ethics.* Harper & Row, 1970, p. 67.
[5]William Stringfellow, *An Ethic for Christians and Other Aliens in a Strange Land.* Word Publishers, 1973, p. 55.

Persons have priority. Those actions are right which sustain the lives of persons. Those relationships are healthy in which persons are nurtured and fulfilled. In seeking clarity about what the "ought" is that makes a legitimate claim on us we rightly ask how we can live in a manner so as to fulfill the lives of others.

The conviction that persons have priority is shared by many who are not consciously inspired by the Christian faith. Much of the recent social protest against the dehumanizing forces in contemporary society has been motivated by a general humanistic concern. In philosophical ethics, a major stream of thought identifies "the good" with what is good for persons. In a discussion of the differences between a Christian and a non-Christian stance in ethics, John Macquarrie points out some fundamental agreements of the two positions on the ultimate goal to be sought:

> Of course, there are often differences of prescription between Christian and non-Christian morals. For instance, Christianity prescribes monogamy, while some other traditions do not. But the question of judging between these prescriptions would be settled by still deeper moral convictions shared by two or more traditions, namely, by seeking which prescription best protects and enhances the true humanity of the persons concerned.[6]

Although the conviction that persons have priority may not be unique to the Christian faith, nevertheless the meaning of this assertion is qualified by the gospel. Let us look briefly at two ways in which the Christian faith gives a distinctive dimension to the priority placed on persons. Then we will seek to understand what it means for Christians to express their faith by putting persons first in their relationships with others.

First, there is a common, and apparently almost universal, appeal to the enhancement of the human as the measure of good. However, this appeal leaves open the question of what it means to be human, of exactly what is the true humanity which is to be protected and enhanced. When an appeal to human values as the good to be sought is followed by specific examples of dehumanization or concrete suggestions for making life more

---

[6]John Macquarrie, *op. cit.,* p. 89.

human, it becomes apparent that various meanings are being given to the concept of human.

For example, the slogan "power to the people" articulates a conviction that there is something dehumanizing to persons when they are powerless. Protests against the war in Vietnam grew, in part, out of the profound conviction that a people whose bodies were burned by napalm and whose fields were destroyed by defoliants were being treated as objects and not as persons. Efforts of women to establish their right to work, to secure loans, or to participate in sports is rooted in the claim that their full personhood can be realized only when they are permitted to use their talents and to assume their responsibilities as fully as men. Concern about prison reform grows out of a conviction that even persons convicted of a crime have fundamental human rights which society is obligated to protect.

Such examples have a powerful appeal as we reflect on what it means to be human. Can anyone deny that full humanity demands the possibility of self-determination, the safety of one's physical existence, the ability to use one's talents and take responsibility, or the protection of one's basic rights and dignity? However, the gospel brings some different dimensions into our consideration of what it means to be human.

Without denying that these insights are important and legitimate, the gospel views human existence in a different perspective. For the Christian, it is Jesus who is the fulfillment of what human existence can be and what God intended it to be. As we seek to understand what it means to give first priority to persons, what is involved in "making and keeping human life human," it is the humanity of Jesus which informs us.

What it meant for Jesus to be human is a basic question which we need to explore in subsequent chapters.

There is a second way in which the Christian faith gives distinctive dimension to the priority placed on persons. While a Christian views human life as a good, the first priority in any ranking of the goods of this world, it is not in and of itself an absolute good. In the perspective of the gospel, our lives are always to be viewed in relation to the eternity and transcendence of God.

The reality of our human situation, viewed in a Christian perspective, is stated most directly in Jesus' response to a scribe's question about which is the greatest commandment:

"The first is, 'Hear, O Israel: The Lord our God, the Lord is one; and you shall love the Lord your God with all your heart, and with all your soul, and with all your mind, and with all your strength.' The second is this, 'You shall love your neighbor as yourself.' There is no other commandment greater than these."

—Mark 12:29-31

Love for the neighbor—concern for the humanity of others, putting persons in the category of top priority—is cited by Jesus as a cardinal commandment. Yet he gives it second place, alongside the commandment to love God. In setting the priorities for the things of this world, we give top priority to persons only after we acknowledge the claims God makes on us. If we set out to do good for our neighbor without paying attention to this first commandment, we get things seriously out of perspective.

What does it mean that Jesus put these two commandments in this way? If we acknowledge that our first response is to love God with all our being, that all of life is to be lived in loving obedience to him, what does it mean for us to give first priority to persons in all of our human relationships? Following are some possible implications.

• To see all of life under God is to become aware of our dependence, and the dependence of others, upon God. We are his creatures. When we deal with ourselves and with others, we are dealing with persons whom God created and about whom God cares. There is a seriousness and an urgency about our efforts to be responsible in our human relationships. For all of us are persons who are known of God, loved of God, and dependent on God.

• To see all of life under God leads us to acknowledge that we are accountable to God. Life is not our own creation; we are not free to do with it solely as we will. Nor are the lives of other persons their creation to do with as they will. All human beings live under the purpose for which God created us. To give persons top priority does not mean that we are obligated to help them do or become whatever they happen to chose.

We seek to discern the will of God for our lives and to help other persons to discern his will for their lives. In both cases the goal is to become the kind of persons God intends us to be.

Precisely what the will of God is for ourselves and for others in specific situations may not be easily discerned. Nevertheless, we are called to seek his will and we are not free simply to do what we want with complete autonomy.

• To see all of life under God brings into focus our own frailty and finiteness. This awareness of our limitations releases us from the awful demands of having to meet all the needs we encounter. We are only human; there is a limit to our strength and our insight. Even though we honestly try to put persons and their needs first in ordering our priorities, we can not do all things for all people.

A young woman who experienced the death of her husband offered this comment: "Why does a person, when confronted by your grief, feel so threatened that he has to prove his worth by being able to fix everything up? What you need is to know they realize the situation for what it is—something that can't be fixed up."

An awareness of our limitations saves us from dogmatic arrogance. Only God is perfectly good. Often we can be mistaken in the good we think we see for ourselves and for others. When we are compelled to take some action, or even to make a decision, we do so with an openness to new perspectives of what is good and with a humility which can make us more sensitive to the real impact of what we are doing.

• To see all of life under God enables us to persist in hope. In our efforts to relate to other persons often we experience disappointments, frustrations, and failures. Some persons will take the good we intend for them and turn it to evil uses. Some will reject the help we offer. Some will persist in making a mess of their lives and ours. Some will fail to take advantage of the chance offered them to become more human. Nevertheless, as we perceive all of life under the transcendence of God, failure to realize the good in our human relationships does not drive us to despair.

We are able to affirm the goodness of God beyond all human good and evil. Thus we dare to believe that, in spite of the failures of his people, God will ultimately realize the good purpose he has for his creation. In this confidence we seek to give first priority to persons in all of our human relationships.

An Enabling Power

In this discussion of the gospel and our priorities, we have made some bold claims. We have asserted that the gospel provides the context in which we set priorities for our life. We have observed that it provides us with directives for setting our priorities. Moreover, we have interpreted the gospel as lifting up a concern for persons as the first priority in our relationships with one another. There is one other claim we need to explore.

As we seek to realize in word and deed our commitment to the Christian faith, we need to be aware of the enabling power of the gospel. This power is to be conceived in personal terms. It is related to the inner life of the individual and is defined in a manner that guards the responsible integrity of the person. As God is known to us in the Christian community, he does not coerce persons to make them good. Rather, he motivates us from within to want to be good and to do good.

The power of the gospel is not an external force which acts apart from the intention and will of the person who wants to make responsible decisions. Neither does the power of the gospel guarantee that we will always know precisely what the good is in every situation. Nor does it offer complete assurance that we will be able to do the good which we discern. Yet the gospel does empower persons to live by the priorities they set for their lives. lives.

The impact of the gospel as an enabling power may be described in several ways.

The gospel helps to shape the lives of persons who experience its transforming power. Its moral precepts have a profound influence on members of the Christian community as they seek to determine how they ought to act in specific situations. Even more significant is the gospel's impact, as James Gustafson points out, "on the formation of the agent, the person, who acts."[7] It influences the fundamental motives and intentions of persons so that they come to desire for themselves the good they discern. cern.

Also persons experience the enabling power of the gospel as they encounter the person of Jesus Christ. Strong individuals in-

---

[7] James Gustafson, *Theology and Christian Ethics.* Pilgrim Press, 1974, p. 148.

fluence any group in which they participate. The presence of any respected individual sets a tone to which others in a community find themselves responding. Jesus makes his influence felt in the Christian fellowship not so much by what he taught as by who he was. To be part of a community in which Jesus is known as the living Lord is to share the subtle impact of his person.

Finally, the gospel offers an enabling power by making persons aware of God's love for them. For a Christian, the moral life is not an heroic achievement of obedience to a set of commandments but rather a response to the grace of God. Our efforts to put priority on the needs of persons is sustained by God's gracious presence with us in worship, prayer, and meditation. To be sure, there is always the struggle with sin which corrupts all human life, but we are empowered by the assurance that God is at work in the lives of his people.

To affirm that the gospel gives priority to persons is to take the first step in our quest to understand how we are to relate responsibly to one another. What this requires of us in specific situations, however, is a matter for serious probing in our continuing discussion.

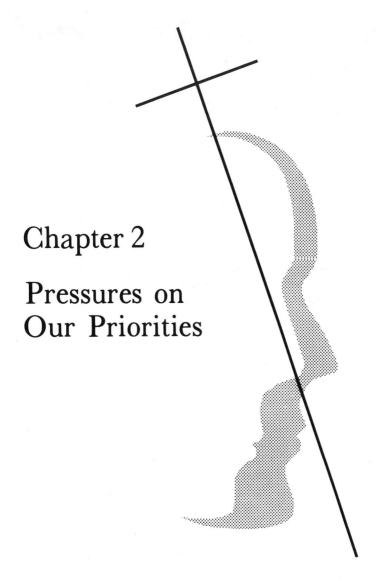

Chapter 2

Pressures on Our Priorities

At certain dramatic moments, the importance of a single human life is vividly demonstrated:

A man tries to fly a balloon across the Atlantic Ocean, and halfway across he disappears. Immediately the resources of the Navy and the Air Force are mobilized. Hundreds of men and thousands of dollars are devoted to finding that one person. A child is kidnapped and the community reacts with profound shock to this threat to a single human life. The parents will put up any amount of money to the limit of their resources in order to recover their child.

A miner is trapped by an explosion hundreds of feet under the ground, and an entire nation watches as every possible effort is made to reach him before his oxygen supply is exhausted.

There are other occasions when the importance of persons is ignored:

A boy comes home eager to tell his father about the camping trip that the Boy Scouts are planning but finds his father so engrossed in reading the newspaper that he just does not seem to be interested in listening.

When a student from a ghetto home fails to understand the homework assignment and does not turn in his work, the teacher makes no effort to help him but simply assumes that he is not interested and cannot do the work anyway.

A mechanic puts a new carburetor in the car he is working on, even though the old carburetor is perfectly good.

A person asks another for her opinion about some work he has done. Because she does not want to offend a friend, she tells him the work is fine even though her honest opinion is that it is not much good.

At a dinner party, a couple dominate the conversation almost entirely, talking about the new house they have just built, the trip they have just taken, the book they are planning to write, or the accomplishments of their children in school.

The neighborhood plans a backyard party and pointedly leaves out the black couple who have recently moved in.

The coach yells and screams at the little leaguer who has just fumbled a ground ball to let the winning run score for the other team.

Instances such as those just mentioned illustrate our sensitivity and callousness to other persons. Although we affirm that persons have priority in our relationships with one another, other priorities sometimes are given a higher rating by our actual response. In fact, our society is often charged with dehumanizing persons in the pursuit of more materialistic values.

William Stringfellow describes dehumanization as "the reversal of dominion between persons and principalities." Following is his caustic indictment of this process.

Specific illustrations of it from contemporary American experience abound—in the precedence, for example, of bureaucratic routine over human need in the administration of welfare or of Medicaid; in the brutalization of inmates where imprisonment is really a means of banishing men from human status, hiding them, treating them as animals or as if they were dead as human beings; in the separation of citizens in apartheid, enforced, as the case may be, by urban housing and development schemes, by racial limitations of access to credit, or by the militia; in the social priorities determined by the momentum of technological proliferation, regardless of either environmental or human interests thereby neglected, damaged, or lost; in genocide practiced for generations against Indian Americans; in the customs of male chauvinism; in the fraud and fakery and the perils to human health and safety sponsored by American merchandising methodology.[1]

Our Other Priorities

What are those other priorities which are being expressed in the actions of people? No exhaustive listing can be made, but we can note some of the things which have been given precedence over a concern for the full well-being of persons.

An obvious alternative to the priority on persons is the priority on money. Whether it be the miserly man who refuses to pay for his children's education because he wants to keep his money, or the major corporation which refuses to invest in the costly safety features for its employees because it wants to keep its profits high, money becomes the value of first importance.

Success may become the supreme good toward which some persons orient their life. It becomes of crucial importance to some persons that they be recognized by the world as men and women who have "made it." To achieve that goal, they are prepared to sacrifice the commitment to spouse, the obligation to family, or the needs of friends.

Power is a priority which sets the pattern of life for many. They have experienced the excitement and satisfaction of exer-

[1]William Stringfellow, *An Ethic for Christians and Other Aliens in a Strange Land.* Word Publishers, 1973, p. 82.

cising power over others, and find the experience so gripping that any means will be used in order to get and keep the prerogatives of power.

Security may become the first order of priority for some people. They find themselves unable to respond to the clear and urgent needs of persons because their first concern is to guard their own situation. Being safe is more important than being helpful.

Group identification often takes precedence over the legitimate claims of persons to be dealt with as individuals, to be accorded their full and unique humanity. The other person cannot be seen or responded to appropriately, becoming simply a member of a group which is different from our group. Or in order to preserve our group, the integrity of persons is denied.

For some people, "doing my thing" becomes the dominant aim of their lives. It does not matter much what their thing is, but whatever it is nothing and no one is going to stand in the way of their doing it. If others have to be ignored or trampled on in order to do their thing, that is unfortunate but that is the way things are going to be.

Life may be dedicated to the goal of having fun, so that whatever gives personal pleasure and satisfaction will be sought, regardless of what the impact of such a quest may be on others.

This brief listing of priorities suggests only a few of the goals and values to which persons may commit themselves. But even this brief listing makes clear that we have many attractive and even compelling alternatives to the option of putting our priority on persons. We misread our situation and underestimate the complexity of our decisions if we assume that the gospel priority on persons is quickly established and easily sustained.

Jesus' Struggle with Priorities

The Christian conviction about the priority on persons issues in significant measure from the teaching of Jesus and the witness of his life. The commitment of his own life is so obvious, and his witness to the priority of persons so consistent, that we may lose the awareness that he too shared with us the struggle to get and to keep his priorities clear. However, the temptation story attests that indeed the goals of his life had to be set by making decisions about real alternatives, alternatives that lured him by their attractiveness.

The temptation story illustrates not only that Jesus too had to struggle to get his priorities straight on persons, but also provides insight into the ways which other priorities can seem to be appropriate, legitimate, even necessary.

The Gospel accounts of his temptations set forth in dramatic fashion the struggle to get his priorities straight, a struggle which must have occupied Jesus repeatedly as he faced the specific circumstances of his ministry. As the Gospels tell the story, Jesus met and turned away the devil right at the beginning of his ministry. Following his baptism he spent forty days in the wilderness. Then the devil came to test him with three temptations.

The devil tempted Jesus to turn stones into bread. The text notes that after forty days without food he was hungry, a picturesque way of declaring what power this temptation must have had for him. Jesus was tempted to give his life to providing for physical needs. The temptation was not only to get food for himself, but also to provide physical food for people and to gain the host of followers who would come to him if he fed them. Jesus did feed great crowds on several occasions, and he fed his disciples at the Last Supper. But the physical food was the symbol of the richer and more profound food which God offers to the whole person.

On one occasion Jesus explicitly warned the people not to mistake the nature of the food which he offered. A crowd came after him, following him even across the sea. But Jesus was not greatly impressed by this display of their interest, for he said to them: "Truly, truly, I say to you, you seek me, not because you saw signs, but because you ate your fill of the loaves. Do not labor for the food which perishes, but for the food which endures to eternal life, which the Son of man will give to you" (John 6:26-27).

Jesus did not live just to feed himself. Although his first concern was for persons, that concern was not defined solely in terms of their physical existence. He did not come to feed people with physical food so they would follow him, but to nurture them with the "food which endures to eternal life."

Then the devil tempted him to seek power and glory over all the world. All Jesus had to do was worship the devil. There must have been occasions when Jesus wanted to grab power so that he could accomplish the goals which he believed to be important. He could establish his kingdom and rid his people of the evil powers which were oppressing them. It would have been so much quicker and easier that way. All he had to do was use some of evil's methods, in order to reach that good goal which he sought.

But Jesus kept his priorities straight. His response to the temptation demonstrates that a concern for persons includes an inescapable concern for the means to be used in the accomplishment of the good. Jesus did not come to get the Kingdom established at any price. He had come for his people and the kingdom of God's love had to be realized within their lives.

Finally, the devil suggested that Jesus jump off the pinnacle of the temple, reminding him that surely God would not let any harm befall him. Such a temptation must have come at Jesus in rather complex ways. As he could have enticed people to follow him by feeding them, so he could have attracted attention by spectacular accomplishments. He could have healed people simply as a demonstration of his marvelous capacity. He could have moved mountains solely to demonstrate his miracle-working powers. Then there must have been occasions when he wanted to test God just to be sure that God was with him, and to make clear to skeptics that he really did have the power of God in his life.

Jesus turned back the enticements of the devil. His first priority was not to get people to follow him but to minister to them. His first priority was not to prove the power of God, but to open the lives of persons so that they could receive the grace and the love which God offered to them.

Jesus' struggle to keep first things first helps us to gain perspective on the ways in which those other priorities will seek to claim us. Several insights are suggested by the way in which Jesus had to deal with his own temptations.

Often we are tempted not by evil in any pure form but by evil under the guise of good. To be sure, there are times when we discern clearly that a course of action is destructive of persons or of relationships, but we do the wrong which we know. More often, however, the temptation to pervert our values and goals confronts us as the claim of a good to be put into the wrong priority.

A value placed in an appropriate ordering of priorities, one in which persons come first, becomes a disvalue when it is placed in a different order. It is good to feed hungry people, but the devil tempted Jesus to put this good as the highest order in his priorities. A look at the list of other priorities noted earlier will confirm that it is good things in their proper order which pressure us to make them more important than persons.

For example, money and many of the things which money can buy are good. The physical possessions which we have can enhance our lives. But the gospel order of priorities gets mixed up when the lives of persons are destroyed in order to secure money, when persons are valued not for themselves but for what they own. The life of a family may be shattered when there is not enough money to provide food, shelter, and heat which persons need. The life of a family also may be destroyed when so much time and energy are devoted to getting possessions that there is no time to create relationships.

Much the same kind of comment could be made about other priorities which were described. The power to determine our own destiny and shape the course of events is a good, but not when gaining that power becomes so important that people are destroyed in the process. We all need a measure of security, but when that need becomes so dominant that it cripples us from running risks on behalf of persons, we have put too much importance on being secure. A sense of our own heritage is vitally significant in giving substance to who we are. But when our identity with a particular group, such as race or nation, prevents us from taking seriously the rights of other persons, the group identity has become a distorting factor in our relationships.

An appeal to our own self-interest is a major force in the distortion of our priorities. The devil kept working at Jesus' personal needs: his need for food, his need for success in his mission, his need for the assurance that God was working with him. Self-interest too is a legitimate good. We do need to be convinced of our own worth, and we do need those things which sustain our lives. But for most of us the problem in our relationships with others is not that we have too little self-interest. Rather we know our own needs and wants so immediately and intensely that they distort our perceptions of the legitimate needs and wants of others.

We want to read the paper after a hard day's work, and so the need of the child to be listened to is ignored. We reason that parents do need to have some time for themselves. We have a hard time making the food budget and are willing to accept the judgment that migrant workers really don't deserve any more than they get. In trying to keep our priorities shaped by the gospel we need to be sensitive to the bias toward self-interest in all our judgments, and be willing to let objective judgments be made when our interests conflict with the interests of others.

The priority of the gospel on persons is not a simple assertion that human physical life is the highest value. Jesus' priority for persons did not mean that he devoted his career to feeding them. When sheer physical survival for ourselves or for others becomes the supreme good, we have distorted the gospel meaning of the priority on persons. Human existence on this earth is a good to be guarded and protected. But Jesus did not spend his days protecting his own life, nor did he concern himself primarily with increasing the number of days which persons spent in this life.

Human physical life is not of absolute value. Many other things have been valued above human life; the honored legends and narratives of the things men have been willing to die for all point to the development of human convictions about things to be valued more than physical life itself—justice, liberty of conscience, exemplary witness to a belief, as well as things valued less highly by most people.[2]

To assert that physical survival of persons is not necessarily the highest priority, either of the gospel or of common human judgment, is not to say that there is a priority higher than persons. It is simply to recognize that persons have dimensions that transcend physical being. If people find other things for which they are willing to die, this means that they have found values which enhance the meaning of being a person.

The final appeal to justify the rightness of a decision is that it is good for persons, not necessarily good for the preservation of physical life but good for whatever it means to be fully human. If we should decide to sacrifice our lives or the lives of others for justice or liberty of conscience, such a decision is grounded in the conviction that for persons to realize the full meaning of their existence, justice and liberty of conscience must be possible. Persons

---

[2]James Gustafson, *Christian Ethics and the Community*. Pilgrim Press, 1971, pp. 140, 142.

do face circumstances when physical survival is subordinated to the greater good of full personhood. And persons do know the pressure to put their own physical survival at the highest priority.

The Anguish of Commitment

The description of Jesus' struggle to get the priorities of his life and ministry straight give some indication of the difficulty all of us have in getting and keeping our priorities straight. Frequently we are tempted to underestimate the difficulty and the costliness of being responsible in our relationships with others, and of keeping the gospel priority clear in what we do. A closer look at the experience of Jesus will add dimension to our understanding of what we face as we try to be faithful.

Jesus is often depicted as a person of power, clarity of purpose, certainty of goal. He spoke with authority. He never faltered in the ministry given to him. He moved with assurance in every situation. The Father gave him a mission which he fulfilled with confidence and courage. But to see Jesus as a man who always knew where he was going and how he was going to get there is to deprive him of the full measure of his humanity. To be human is to have moments of uncertainty when we are not sure of our direction or whether we have the strength to go on.

The temptation story points to tough questions which Jesus had to struggle with in his ministry. Those questions were not easily answered, for only out of days of pondering, fasting, and living with the Scriptures did Jesus get clear on the priorities of his life.

The scene in the garden of Gethsemane near the end of his life gives another glimpse into the inner turmoil which was part of his experience. (See Mark 14:32-42; Matt. 26:36-46; Luke 22:40-46.) He knew that the time of crisis had come. His enemies were about to take him, and he foresaw that they would kill him. At this moment he still had a decision to make, whether he would escape from those who sought his life or whether he would stay on the course which had brought him to this danger.

This scene gives evidence of the awful anguish which Jesus experienced at this crisis moment in his life. Luke gives a particularly vivid picture: ''And being in an agony he prayed more earnestly; and his sweat became like great drops of blood falling down upon the ground" (Luke 22:43). Matthew describes how he fell on his face and prayed, and how he returned three times to pray. Clearly Jesus was in the throes of a serious struggle, seeking to know what his commitment meant, seeking to know what he should do, seeking to find the strength to do whatever might be set before him.

We can understand something of the pressures which were on him and of the questions which troubled him. He must have found some difficulty in dealing with the fact that he had encountered opposition from the religious leaders of his own people. The priests, the scribes, and the Pharisees denounced him bitterly. To have such an array of learning and authority set against him must have forced him to ponder whether he was right or whether they were right in their discernment of what God really intended for his people.

He must have hesitated at the price he was being asked to pay for his effort to affirm the way of God and to minister to persons. Jesus knew that the way he had chosen was dangerous. He was quite aware that he had offended powerful people. He warned his disciples repeatedly that he faced death when he went to Jerusalem. As the time actually came when he was going to be arrested, the prospect of his suffering and death must have struck him with terrible impact. The possibility of forgetting about his responsibility to people and fleeing to some quiet corner to live out his days in peace must have seemed attractive indeed. So he would pray: "My Father, if it be possible, let this cup pass from me" (Matt. 26:39).

Jesus must have pondered what it meant that people seemed to have so misunderstood what he was trying to do. People had hailed him when he entered Jerusalem a few days earlier, but many of them were looking for a messiah who would come with power to overthrow the Roman rulers. For a time great crowds followed him, but that was in the days when he was feeding the people and healing the sick. They wanted the good *things* he could give to them but not the good *news* he was bringing to them.

Even his disciples did not seem to grasp what it was all about. James and John asked for the best seats in the kingdom. The other disciples got upset because they feared they might lose out on the best seats. Peter called him messiah but showed he did not really understand. Jesus must have asked himself if dying for what he believed in was worth it when people missed the whole point of what he was doing.

Finally, the loneliness and isolation must have put terrible pressure on Jesus as he struggled to know what he should do. The people he had tried to help had all left him. Even the disciples would leave him. They could not stay awake to pray with him, and Peter would deny him three times before the night was over. Jesus found himself alone, alone with his commitment to God, alone with his commitment to minister to people in God's name.

How difficult it is to stand alone. In times of stress and hard decision, it is a source of strength to have even one other person to share the burden.

Jesus in Gethsemane was "sorrowful and troubled." If he had not cared profoundly for people, his decision would have been easy. He would have gone back home to forget the whole unhappy business. The sight of Jesus in the garden of Gethsemane helps us to be aware of the intensity of the pressures to change our priorities and to deny the values which the gospel affirms for us. We would all like to live in a world in which the right thing is the easy thing. But that is not the kind of world we live in.

Thousands of Americans experienced the anguish of commitment due to their refusal to participate in the war in Vietnam. Convinced that the war was wrong and a violation of fundamental human decency, they refused to be drafted or left the military service. This decision forced many of them to flee to Canada or Sweden and live as aliens in a strange community. The full weight of the leadership of their government was thrown against them. In many instances their families and those closest to them, who did not share their decision of conscience, disowned them. For the moment, and perhaps forever, they have been cut off from sharing in the community which nurtured them.

Not all decision to do the good as we see it will be as traumatic or have such profound implications as the decisions made by those who refused to serve in Vietnam. But we may be sure that if we truly put our priority on persons there will be times when faithfulness to that commitment will bring anguished decisions.

For example, an employee's protest against the company practice of finding ways to void warranties may result in service penalties, but a protest may have to be made if there is honest concern about the people whose needs are not being met because of faulty products. Befriending a person whose style of life makes him an outcast in a group may mean taking ridicule and loss of status for oneself. Public support for a measure designed to protect the poor from being exploited by housing interests may bring threats of retribution.

Each of us will face in our unique circumstances those situations when we are pressed to move from the gospel priority on persons. Money and success and power and all those other goods are important to us, and there will be times when they push our concern for persons aside. But, by the grace of God, there will also be times when we will suffer the anguish to be faithful in our commitment to the welfare of persons.

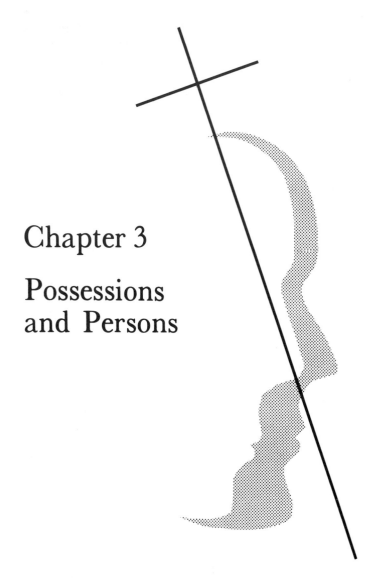

Chapter 3

Possessions and Persons

A walk through a department store confronts us with an astonishing array of things. Before we even get to the store, advertisers have presented us with pictures and descriptions of an almost unlimited number of things which they are urging us to buy. Each year researchers and inventors come up with hundreds of new items to put on the market in the hope that enough of us will buy them so that business people can make a profit.

How does modern merchandising influence our judgment in regard to setting priorities? In what ways does the enticement to own and possess things distort our perspective of life's basic values? How do possessions tempt us to give them first place in our lives?

In this chapter we continue our discussion of the temptations we face to place other priorities above the needs of persons. We have noted that the gospel affirms that a concern for persons is the highest priority in responsible Christian living. How can we keep possessions and persons in proper perspective?

Appeal of Possessions

Why are possessions so appealing to us? What enticements lure us to spend our limited resources on things? Why is it such a struggle for us to keep possessions in their proper perspective?

Things are offered to us because they are useful. As physical creatures we use many kinds of physical possessions simply to maintain life. For example, no matter how spare we try to be, we all need food and clothing and shelter. Such possessions are important because they are an absolute necessity. If we could simply reject all physical objects and material things we could solve the problem of keeping them in proper perspective with ease. But we cannot flatly reject them. Therefore we must struggle constantly to keep them from becoming too dominant in the total complex of goods and values.

Things are offered to us because they are attractive and will make living more attractive. Curtains and pictures and records are not essential to maintain physical existence, but they add beauty and grace. Or, things are offered to us because they will make us more attractive personally. A necktie or an earring are decorative objects which add a touch of color. Can we do without things which make our surroundings beautiful and add a touch of color to us personally? How do we weigh the value of things which add aesthetic beauty to our lives against the value of things which would give greater physical health to others?

The few people who have had the opportunity to visit mainland China in recent years have often noted the drabness of the appearance of the people. They have noted an apparent lack of crunching poverty. The resources of that controlled society are not used for the aesthetic "frills" for some but for the fundamental needs of all. We would not want to exchange all of the color and beauty in our lives for the drabness we see at least externally in Chinese society. Yet in conscience we have to ask what kind of priorities we have when we spend vast sums for cosmetics and there are children in our midst whose lives are stunted because they do not have enough to eat.

Things are offered to appeal to our need for protection from threat or danger. A lock on the door, a chain on the bicycle, a seat belt in the car, a railing around the porch—these are designed for our personal safety or to guard against the loss of the possessions we have. In the complex and impersonal urban society in which we live, the need for things to protect not only our other possessions but even our lives grows increasingly urgent.

Things are offered to appeal to our desire to express our affection for others. There are cards to send at Christmas, and candies for Valentine's Day, and gifts for a birthday, and flowers for Mother's Day, and ties for Father's Day. Physical objects can express in meaningful fashion the affection which we have for others. Giving gifts is a tangible way in which we can manifest our feelings for others, feelings which we often find difficult to articulate in words.

Things are offered to appeal to our desire for recreation. With the increasing leisure time available to persons in our society, possessions designed for recreation have proliferated. We are confronted with an apparently endless array of things to help us have fun—games, boats, skis, snowmobiles, golf clubs, fishing tackle, toys, footballs, tennis racquets. And with the increasing leisure time available the quality of life in growing measure depends on the capacity to make good use of the time and the things available for our recreation.

Things are offered to enable us to be mobile. In our culture, mobility is an asset. We would find it very difficult to function, to carry on our work, and to relate to people, if we did not have the capacity to move with speed and on an individual basis. It is the car which makes both speed and individual movement possible. The housing patterns and employment patterns into which most of us have to fit simply demand that we have the things which make it possible for us to move.

Things are offered to appeal to our desire for ease and comfort. For most of us, survival does not depend on the air-conditioner or the vacuum cleaner or the washing machine, but such things make life considerably more pleasant. Labor-saving devices can be justified as they give persons the time and energy to do more creative things than dusting the house or washing the clothes.

Things are offered to appeal to our desire to improve ourselves. Books and tape recorders and maps and newspapers and television sets will give information which will make us more adequate to deal with the complexity of our world.

Things are offered to appeal to our desire for prestige or status or meaning. A car is not merely a means of transportation but is offered as a way of creating a certain image. A bigger house in the right neighborhood will provide not only more space for a growing family but the prestige associated with the right address.

Things are offered to appeal to our desire to own something of value. Diamonds, fine paintings, land, and sterling silver provide us with something of value and something which has the promise of keeping its value.

Because possessions are such an important part of our lives and have so many functions, it is understandable that dealing with possessions consumes so much attention and poses difficult decisions. Earlier we talked about how material things can add beauty to our lives. We wondered about what kind of priorities would justify spending huge sums for beauty aids while some persons in our midst live near starvation. Similar questions can be raised abut all the other functions which physical objects have in our lives. How much of our resources, for example, should we spend to get the things needed to protect the things we already have? If we spent more of our resources meeting the physical, psychological, and spiritual needs of people who steal, would we need to spend so much defending ourselves against them?

Things can be a way of expressing concern and love which persons have for each other, but at what point do these things become a substitute for the more personal expression of genuine affection? Things do help us to fill our leisure and have our fun, but how do we guard against the risk that filling our leisure with "fun things" will cripple our capacity for creative use of the time to do what we want? Things can be justified as they free persons from the terrible drudgery of routine and boring tasks, but to what limit do we go in getting things solely for the purpose of making life pleasant and easy?

People find meaning and value in the objects they possess, but at what point does the lodging of meaning in their possessions deprive them of the richer meanings which life can offer? Things are important for sustaining and nurturing lives, but how do persons protect themselves against the threat of becoming slaves to the things they own?

There are no simple, precise answers to such questions, but they are significant questions with which we must deal. The appeal to get more possessions is constantly at work on us. With every acquisition of a thing there is an expression of our priorities. Our use of possessions says much about the kind of person we are and has profound implications for the relationshps which we have with others.

Attitudes Towards Possessions

A Christian perspective on life and the world offers some insight into the way we gain and use our possessions, but the gospel does not offer any neat solutions or easy answers. There have been some neat solutions put forth as "the Christian way" to deal with possessions. As illustration of these solutions, we might note two extreme positions which have been actually expressed in the lives of persons who have been trying to be faithful to their understanding of what the Christian faith demanded of them.

At one extreme have been those who have renounced all possessions and reduced to a bare minimum the things they used. St. Francis of Assisi is a notable example of those who have tried to be obedient to God and loyal to Jesus Christ by renouncing the goods of this world. Many have preceded him and many have followed his example. Throughout the history of the church, the vow of poverty has been one of the significant commitments persons have made in response to Jesus as Lord.

But the questions about possessions persist. What is the absolutely bare minimum? Is it a violation of a vow of poverty to have an object of beauty? Are people who have to deal with possessions, and who make decisions about them to get the world's work done, lesser Christians than those who withdraw from this responsibility? Is it more Christian to beg for the food one needs than to work for it?

At the other extreme there have been those who have believed that the Christian faith is a guarantee of success and prosperity, defined in terms of the acquisition of possessions. This view is illustrated in the comment of a retired Chicago banker: "We pray . . . to do the right thing, because the right thing is usually the profitable thing, too. We want God to show us the right way to success."[1] Prosperity is the sign of God's blessing. Possessions and power are given to those whom God chooses. This is an interpretation of the human situation which leads easily to the view that those who have wealth are superior in God's sight to those who do not, that those who have possessions have a God-given right to do with them whatever they choose.

According to the biblical witness, neither of these extremes is normative for the Christian view of possessions. Jesus was not an ascetic. He did not withdraw nor isolate himself from the world. At one point he had to deal with the charge that he used the things of the world too much. "The Son of man has come eating and drinking; and you say, 'Behold, a glutton and a drunkard, a friend of tax collectors and sinners' " (Luke 7:34).

To be sure, he did not acquire a big house and vast properties, but he was concerned about the physical well-being of people: about their health, about their need for shelter, about their need for food. The attitude of Jesus is consonant with the broader biblical perspective which sees the physical world not as evil, but as God's creation and his gift.

Nevertheless, Jesus had severe words to speak about the dangers of wealth and possessions. He told a parable about a rich fool who accumulated so much that he had to build bigger barns to hold it. It would appear that the rich man had two problems. First, he had so little imagination he could not think of anything to do with all his wealth except to build bigger barns to store it. Second, he thought that his life was going to be rich and full because he had an abundance of possessions and he could take it easy. At the moment he thought that, God said to him, "Fool! This night your soul is required of you; and the things you have

---

[1]Quoted in *The Christian Century*, June 13-20, 1973, p. 680.

prepared, whose will they be?" (Luke 12:20). The problem of the rich man was not that he had great possessions, but that he didn't know what to do with them.

Repeatedly, Jesus indicated his concern when possessions seemed to loom too large in a person's perspective on life and its meaning. That appeared to be the problem of the ruler who came to ask Jesus what he must do to inherit eternal life. He was obviously a good man, for he had kept all the commandments and was concerned about the life eternal. But Jesus perceived that he depended too heavily on his possessions, that they were simply too important to him.

Jesus told this man: "Sell all that you have and distribute to the poor, and you will have treasure in heaven; and come, follow me." Then comes one of the saddest sentences in all the Scriptures: "But when he heard this he became sad, for he was very rich" (Luke 18:22-23).

Jesus knew the value of possessions, but he also knew the limitation and danger of possessions. Possessions do not give life. The person who looks to things for meaning and fulfillment will be sorely disappointed.

It is easy to believe that security lies in wealth, for people who have wealth are indeed protected against many of the threats which plague the poor. But wealth does not give the only ultimate and meaningful security, which is the certainty of God's love for his people. Because possessions loom so large in human existence, they can distort judgments until it seems that people are important simply because of what they own.

Surely from a Christian perspective and the biblical witness there is great value in possessions. They not only enable persons to sustain their lives, but they provide the resources which enables them to give alms to the poor, to feed the hungry, to clothe the naked. But the Christian faith also offers insight into the dangers of possessions and our use of them. We are always tempted to put too much emphasis on things and to give too high a priority to possessions.

Possessions in Perspective

Possessions have many functions in our lives, from providing the physical necessities for sustaining life to adding the beauty which enriches our existence. The decisions we must make about acquiring and using possessions pose serious problems if we are to be responsible to the gospel priority on persons. We cannot simplify those decisions, either by getting rid of our possessions or by equating them with the good. But the gospel does give a perspective which helps us in the struggle to keep our possessions in the proper priority.

First, we are constantly tempted to overemphasize our own wants in weighing our desire for things against the needs of others. Every expenditure for ourselves is a decision to use our resources for our own needs rather than in ministry to other persons. The gospel helps to make us aware of how self-centered we can become, and enables us as responsible persons to make a conscious effort to balance that bias so that our use of possessions reflects a genuine priority on persons.

Second, the gospel not only recognizes that possessions are necessary for life and expresses a concern that persons have those necessities which make full human existence possible. It also asserts that having things is not to be equated with life.

If there is a floor of having below which it is hard or impossible to be fully human, I wonder if there may not also be a ceiling of having above which a genuinely human existence becomes very difficult. . . . If there is a poverty that dehumanizes, there is also an affluence or acquisitiveness that dehumanizes, though in a different manner. Man must have something in order to be something; but there is no simple correlation between the extent of his having and the depth of his being.[2]

Under the impact of the Christian faith we will be clear that possessions for ourselves and for others are a prerequisite of full human life, but they are not the source or the meaning of that life. Therefore, we will not invest things with an importance beyond their subsidiary role.

Third, we will not equate the giving of things with the expressing of concern. To be sure, in many circumstances the only way in which we can manifest our priority for persons is by giving money or goods. When a drought brings desperate famine to Africa or an earthquake devastates Peru, money and food and

---

[2] John Macquarrie, *Three Issues in Ethics*. Harper & Row, 1970, p. 58.

medical supplies are what people need. But the gift of a toy from a parent is no substitute for willingness to take time and energy to listen to and be with the child. An expensive Christmas gift to the secretary does not rectify the wrong of total insensitivity to his or her personal feelings during the rest of the year.

In innumerable ways we face the issue of whether persons or possessions will have priority. Will the church allow the use of its newly decorated building by a Scout troop? Will the town use tax money to provide a youth center and a program? Is the bigger salary of a promotion worth the disruption of home and family which the move will bring? We need to bring all the power and the perspective given by the gospel to our difficult task of dealing with our possessions.

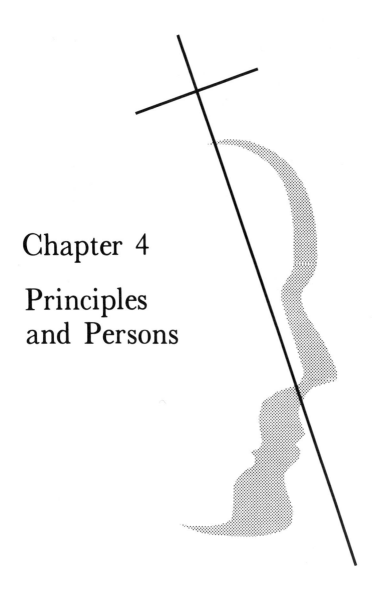

Chapter 4

Principles and Persons

All of us live in a community of persons whose relationships with one another are subject to a complex network of rules, regulations, laws, commandments, customs, and mores. Families have rules about how their children are to behave, and parents are subject to legal restrictions about how they treat their children. Institutions adopt constitutions and by-laws which specify how their members are to function. Neighborhoods set certain standards or customs which the residents are expected to observe. Societies have legislative bodies which set forth laws, executives who enforce the laws, and courts which interpret the laws and punish persons who violate them.

In the Christian fellowship we are also governed by a set of principles derived from our heritage of biblical faith. These may be referred to as the laws of God, divine commandments, beatitudes, guidelines for Christian living, or church discipline. Basically, what we are concerned with here are those standards of right and wrong, good and evil, which Christians accept as guides to human behavior.

How are our relationships with one another shaped by all of these laws, regulations, customs, and principles of the society in which we live? What difficulties do they present as we struggle to give first priority to the needs of persons? What is the proper role of principles in the ordering of our priorities?

Our Need for Principles

Laws, rules, and mores serve crucial functions in human society. Laws enable many people to live together in a limited space. If there were no laws about how motor vehicles were to be operated, the roads would be complete chaos and no one could move. It is the mores about how persons are to behave and to carry on their life which shapes a community and enables individuals to function as members of the larger body. Laws define the rights of people and set forth how those rights shall be respected in relationship to other people.

Laws and rules help persons to know what is expected of them and what is appropriate behavior in their relations with others. Principles of right and wrong express the consensus of the community about what is proper moral behavior. Laws enable a community or a nation to provide the facilities and resources necessary for the common good. Laws provide ways for society to deal with those persons who pose a threat to the health and the safety of others. Generally accepted standards of right and wrong enable persons to approach moral decisions with some sense of what the human community has judged to be appropriate behavior.

The concept of the law of God articulates the conviction that God has established standards of how persons shall deal with one another in appropriate ways. The laws which govern human relationships and the principles of right and wrong are not simply the distillation of human experience. God the Creator has built into the fabric of his creation the moral imperatives which are made known to his people as the laws of God.

The laws of the society, the principles of right and wrong, the mores of the community—all these can be supported and justified on the grounds that they benefit the lives of persons. Human community would not be possible at all without law, and where the law has been weakened persons have suffered. The quality of life has been diminished when the vital impact of moral principles has been weakened.

It was with considerable justification that many people viewed with alarm what they regarded as easy calls for disobedience to the law during the civil rights protests and the war protests of the 1960s. They saw seeds of anarchy being sown, and rightly viewed with great fear the prospect of reaping that harvest. Also the Watergate affair involved many issues of political practice, national security, separation of power in United States government, style of leadership, campaign financing, press responsibility, and rights to privacy. But the fundamental issue focused on whether or not this was to be a government of law to which all persons are subject. It became clear that the decision on that issue had a profound impact on the future of the United States. The increase in crime in this country has brought understandable cries for increased police power to restore law and order to communities. For the quality of life is sadly diminished when the law is violated by so many with such impunity. Human existence is impoverished when persons sit alone in their houses because they fear to walk the streets, when barricades have to be built to protect life and property, when every stranger is not a new possibility for a unique relationship but a danger.

Principles, in the broad meaning of the term, are absolutely crucial for human existence.

Limitations of Principles

If the law is necessary for persons to live together, the law also has its limitations when the full range of human relationships is considered. Although principles help persons to be responsible, they are not a full and complete guide to the ways in which persons ought to deal with one another. Principles are good, but they are neither adequate nor absolute. "To treat past or present lists of 'do's' and 'don'ts' as completely inflexible is to make them ends in themselves, and is an idolatry which does irreparable harm to persons, physically, mentally, and spiritually."[1]

Principles cannot force persons to do the creative, the generous, the loving action. The law defines the rights of persons which must be respected. But beyond these rights there are the needs of persons which can be met only in generous and compassionate acts. These the law cannot demand.

Principles cannot force the motivations with which persons act toward one another. The law does deal in motives, of course. When one person has killed another, it is significant before the law to determine whether the act was premeditated or in self-defense. The law can require that a person act in a certain way, but the law cannot demand that a person act with a particular motivation. Relationships between persons may be legally quite correct, and at the same time be bitter and destructive because of the spirit in which the persons deal with each other.

In considering the laws and rules which society establishes, it must be recognized that they are creations of persons, and therefore fallible and corruptible. The laws we make may not be just to all members of the society. Certain groups may be denied their rightful protection, and other groups may use the laws to their own gain at the expense of others. Situations change, and laws which were once appropriate may become inappropriate. Although the Christian faith affirms the biblical witness to the law of God, the meaning of that law and the specifics of that law are interpreted by persons with their own biases and perspectives which are limited by the particular historical situation.

---

[1]O. Sydney Barr, *The Christian New Morality*. Oxford University Press, 1969, p. 12.

Laws, rules, and regulations cannot cover every contingency, nor prescribe for the distinctive character of every relationship. Beyond what the law demands and the rules specify, responsible action demands a capacity to deal with others in situations where there is no specific guidance.

Principles, like possessions, are necessary for the welfare of persons, and yet they must be subservient to the priority on persons. There are important standards of right and wrong which guide us as we seek to deal responsibly with others. There are accepted ways of doing things which make it easier for us to maintain relationships with others. There are laws which prescribe responsible behavior in society. However, there are times when the needs of persons take precedence over laws and rules.

How Jesus Interpreted Principles

The way Jesus dealt with demands of the law and obligations imposed by principles gives us an insight into the priority which the gospel assigns to persons. Moreover, his example offers us a model for dealing with the difficult task of relating the needs of persons to the demands of the law.

On many occasions Jesus ran into conflict with the religious authorities of his people, primarily because of a difference in attitudes toward the law. Crucial issues were at stake in his struggles with the scribes and Pharisees. Conflicts arose when Jesus, or his disciples, violated a specific prohibition of the law.

One Sabbath, for example, Jesus' disciples picked some grain as they traveled through a field. This act was a common practice of the time, but to pick grain on the sabbath was a violation of the laws governing the sabbath. The Pharisees complained: "Look, your disciples are doing what is not lawful to do on the sabbath" (Matt. 12:2). Jesus responded by citing an incident from the Old Testament when David and his men were hungry. They came to the House of God where they found bread which could be eaten only by priests, but because of their need David took the bread and gave it to his men. On other occasions Jesus healed on the sabbath, and was rebuked because healing also was defined as work. In each case he defended himself on the ground that the need of the person justified his acting contrary to the law.

Jesus summed up his attitude toward the sabbath and its rules in the assertion that "The sabbath was made for man, not man for the sabbath; so the Son of man is lord even of the sabbath" (Mark 2:27-28). He recognized the value of the day set aside for rest and for worship, a day of reminder that God is the Creator who rested on the seventh day. Jesus did not deny the importance of rules and laws to help people use the sabbath well. But he contended that the needs of persons were more important than obedience to the law prescribing how the sabbath was to be observed. The law of the sabbath in itself was not significant; it had meaning only as it contributed to the total welfare of persons.

In another encounter with the Pharisees and scribes Jesus faced a different kind of issue. They complained: "Why do your disciples transgress the tradition of the elders? For they do not wash their hands when they eat" (Matt. 15:2). The rules about ceremonial washing of hands was not even a law, but a "tradition of the elders."

Jesus responded by charging that the Pharisees transgressed the commandments of God for the sake of their tradition. The tradition, for example, allowed a person to pledge part of his property to God. When a person had made such a pledge he could continue using the property for himself, and furthermore he did not have to use any of it to support his parents. Here was a situation in which adherence to a tradition, or a custom, was used to escape what Jesus viewed as the more significant responsibility of concern for parents.

Not all rules are of equal significance, and the significance of a law is determined by its impact on the welfare of persons. Jesus' judgment about the way the scribes and Pharisees misused the law is summed up in the charge: "You tithe mint and dill and cummin, and have neglected the weightier matters of the law, justice and mercy and faith" (Matt. 23:23). The law required a tithe, and the tradition said that the tithe had to be paid of even the small herbs, mint and dill and cummin. The scribes and Pharisees were rigorous in their insistence on the payment of this tithe, but in the meantime they neglected what Jesus believed to be far more important, justice and mercy and faith.

One of Jesus' parables (Matt. 20:1-16) has significant implications for our reflection on the role of principles in human relationships. The story is about the owner of a vineyard who hires a group of workers at the beginning of the day and agrees with them on the amount they are to be paid. Several times throughout the day, he hires other workers whom he finds standing idle in the marketplace. Near the close of the day, he hires some who work only one hour. At quitting time, he pays all of the workers the same wage.

The first workers, those "who have borne the burden of the day and the scorching heat," begin to grumble that they are being treated unjustly. The owner of the vineyard reminds them that they have received the wages agreed upon. Nevertheless, they feel they should have received more pay than the workers who labored only one hour.

We can understand the discontent of those first workers. If an employer today were to deal with his employees in this manner, he might quickly find himself in trouble with a union. The behavior of the vineyard owner violates the fundamental principle of equality which we have come to accept in human relationships. All persons should be dealt with equally. On any specific job, workers should be paid according to the amount of time they have worked.

What message did Jesus intend to convey in telling this parable? Notice that he offered it as a description of what the kingdom of heaven is like. Obviously, we miss the point if we interpret it to be a manual on labor relations. He is talking about how God deals with his people, about God's boundless generosity and concern for every person. It is this emphasis that has implications for the way we deal with one another.

The story vividly suggests that the principle of equality is not the only consideration involved in human relationships. The owner of the vineyard fulfilled his agreement with the first workers in regard to their pay. Out of his generosity he gave all the laborers a full day's wage. The last workers hired, even though they worked only one hour, had the same needs as the others for food, clothing, and shelter. Was it really an injustice to the first workers hired to give priority to the needs of persons rather than to the principle of equal wages for equal work?

Jesus summarized his perspective of the law and rules and principles in the passage we know as the Sermon on the Mount. "Think not that I have come to abolish the law and the prophets; I have come not to abolish them but to fulfill them. . . . For I tell you, unless your righteousness exceeds that of the scribes and Pharisees, you will never enter the kingdom of heaven" (Matt. 5:17, 20).

He did not come to overthrow the law or do away with it. The law was the law of God, and keeping the law was closely connected with a person's relationship to the kingdom of heaven. But if Jesus did not come to abolish the law, neither did he come to leave the law just as it was. For the scribes and Pharisees particularly the law specified every aspect of conduct, and obedience to every detail of the law was the way to righteousness. Jesus valued the law, but he came to fulfill the law.

Two examples are offered to illustrate what he meant by saying he came to fulfill the law. The law said do not kill, but Jesus pointed out that anger toward a brother is destructive of the relationship with him. The law said do not commit adultery, but Jesus pointed out that lust, even without the overt act, is adultery. The law dealt with actions, but Jesus was concerned about the subtler dimensions of human relationships.

The fulfillment of the law in Jesus related the concern and obligation in our dealings with others not only to what we do, but to our attitudes and feelings. To kill one's brother is an obvious denial of his humanity but so also is anger. To commit adultery is a violation of commitments made and a using of persons for one's own ends but so also is lust.

As Jesus dealt with the role of principles in responsible human relationships, in every instance where the demands of the law conflicted with the needs of a person, the needs of the person took precedence. Where the law was not sufficient to lead people to true righteousness, Jesus pointed to the significance of creative and loving relationships. Where the lesser demands of the law conflicted with justice and mercy, it was justice and mercy to which Jesus called persons.

Principles in Perspective

We have stated in this chapter that principles, using a broad definition of that term, have a legitimate priority in human affairs because they serve to further and protect the welfare of persons. But principles do not have an absolute priority. There are occasions when laws and customs, rules, and mores, will be set aside because of the higher priority given to persons.

Setting aside principles because the higher claim of persons demands it is never done easily or lightly. Sometimes, however, it must be done if our prime concern is what happens to people. Under the impact of the gospel we seek to order our relationships with others on the basis of seeking their welfare rather than on the basis of upholding important principles.

A look at some specific situations will serve to alert us to the difficulties and ambiguities confronting us as we try to give an appropriate priority to principles at the same time that we give first priority to persons. One biblical example will help to raise some of the issues involved.

Soon after the death and resurrection of Jesus, Peter was deeply involved in the witness and ministry of the early Christian community. One day he received an appeal from Cornelius, a Roman officer, to come to his house. It was with great reluctance that Peter went, for as he told Cornelius when he got there: "You yourselves know how unlawful it is for a Jew to associate with or to visit any one of another nation" (Acts 10:28). In fact, it took a vision of the heavens opening and a direct command from the Spirit to get Peter to move. Deep within him was the conviction that the law required a Jew to keep separate from the Gentiles.

Peter was also quite aware that by going to the home of a Roman officer he was leaving himself wide open to criticism from his fellow Jews. The principle of maintaining the purity of the people of God was a powerful and gripping compulsion of the Jewish people, a principle which was crucially significant in their capacity to survive as a people. So Peter did not violate easily that law which forbad him to relate to a person of another nation.

It took a good deal of dramatic evidence to persuade him, but Peter finally became convinced that the needs of Cornelius and his family for the ministry of Jesus Christ outweighed the rule and regulation designed to guard the purity of the people of God. So Peter went to Cornelius, entered his house, preached to him the good news of Jesus Christ, and baptized him and his household. The needs of a person took priority over what Peter understood to be the demands of the law of God.

In a variety of circumstances we may have to decide whether concern for a person outweighs the value of holding on to a deeply held conviction. For example, parents who have strong convictions about sexual morality must decide how to respond when a daughter proposes to move in with a young man at college and wants to share her room with him while they are at home on vacation. After the parents have expressed their conviction that for her own fulfillment as a person such sexual relationships are inadequate, what do they do when she persists? Should they cut off support for her education? Or should they accept the living arrangement she has made at school, but refuse to allow them to live together in their daughter's own home? Should they welcome them when they come home together?

The decision is not easy. It is difficult for parents to sort out whether they are reacting to an offense to their own deeply held standards, or whether they are reacting out of genuine concern for the welfare of their daughter. If they accept the arrangement she proposes, are they failing in their responsibility to her to uphold standards which she herself may want to hold but is too weak to do so under the pressures she experiences? If they refuse to allow the arrangement, are they in danger of breaking off a precious personal relationship because of their refusal to compromise on a principle?

From the gospel perspective, the first priority is concern for their daughter, and not for upholding a principle or ministering to their own hurt feelings. But how that concern is to be expressed will be grasped only with profound sensitivity to the delicate nuances of their daughter's identity and their relationships with her.

Another example poses different issues. On a number of occasions in our recent history, persons have deliberately disobeyed the law out of conviction that a higher allegiance to the needs of persons demanded such a course. During the time of civil rights activism, large numbers of people were arrested as they protested segregation in schools, stores, parks, and swimming pools by disobeying laws which established segregated facilities. During the Vietnam war, people protested by tearing up their draft cards, by sitting in public buildings after they had been ordered to move, by breaking in to draft board offices and destroying records.

Such tactics were obviously controversial. On the one hand, there were those who argued that any willful disobedience of the law is a threat to the whole society and weakens the fabric of our common life. If one person can break the law for what he or she considers a good cause, cannot all persons do the same? When persons have the right to decide what laws they will or will not obey, anarchy is the result. Furthermore, there are means in our society by which laws that are inadequate or unjust can be changed through the orderly means provided.

On the other hand, there were those who believed that the law itself had become an instrument of repression and evil. The law was the tool of the white community to oppress the black community. The evil of the war was so monstrous that any means to protest against it was justified. Legal protests had failed to change the policy of the nation. Innocent people were being killed daily in a war which had no legal or moral justification.

Those who protested by civil disobedience could claim that it was for no personal gain, and that they were willing to accept the consequences of their actions. They did not break the law in secret in order to escape punishment, but in public in order to dramatize by their arrest the cause in which they believed deeply.

Laws, rules, mores, and customs have a high priority because they are significant in preserving life and making meaningful relationships between persons possible. But their claim on us is not absolute. Under the impact of the gospel, we sometimes have the awesome responsibility of deciding that in specific circumstances the needs of persons have precedence over the priority of principles.

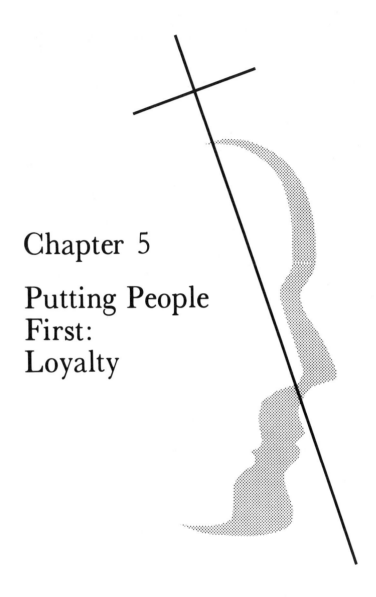

Chapter 5

Putting People First: Loyalty

Commitment to Jesus Christ and acceptance of the gospel embodied in him shape the way we deal with others. Under the impact of the gospel we are moved so to act that people come first. We are concerned about making and keeping life human, about meeting the real needs of persons, about enabling persons to fulfill their potential. As we have seen there are many alternative priorities which fight for precedence as we make the big and small decisions of our lives. But faithfulness to the gospel in our human relationships means that persons have priority.

To affirm the priority on persons as the guide for responsible and ethical Christian relationships is important, for until we get our priorities straightened out we are surely in great confusion. But to affirm the priority on persons does not solve all the problems we face in specific situations. Just what does it mean to put people first? It is to that question that we now turn to explore in detail in the next several chapters some of the ways our primary concern for persons gets expressed as we actually live with others.

Loyalty to others is one manifestation of our concern for them. We will consider now what it means for us to seek to be loyal in our relationships.

Loyalty to Persons

Life is a continual running into, responding to, and dealing with a host of other people. When we really begin to take note of all the people with whom we have some kind of relationship, it turns out to be an impressive number.

In the ordinary routine of our days we have contact with clerks in the store, policemen who direct traffic, members of our family, drivers of the cars we meet on the street, friends, salespersons who call us on the phone, telephone operators, business associates, truck drivers, deliverers of our newspapers, doctors, janitors, neighbors and their children, and many other persons. Beyond the people we actually meet physically, there are countless numbers who have some impact on our lives, or who are influenced in some way by what we do. We may never meet the persons who write the editorials, keep the traffic lights operating, plan the school curriculum, control the air traffic patterns, but they are important and what they do makes a difference to us.

To be concerned about the persons we meet or with whom we have some kind of interaction is to be loyal to those persons in fulfilling the obligations which are attendant upon that relationship. To put people first is to be loyal to them, but not every encounter with another person has equal significance or carries the same obligation. The touching of hands by two people who are engaged means something quite different from the quick touch when a salesperson hands over a small object. The relationship of two drivers passing on the highway is different from the relationship of two persons who have shared life together for forty years.

Our lives are a complex network of loyalties. What it means to be loyal in any particular circumstance depends on a number of factors which influence the meaning of this relationship.

• *The length of the relationship.* There is no absolute correlation between the length of time people have known each other and the seriousness of their obligation toward each other. Two persons can have known each other for many years and never have developed significant dimensions in their contacts. However, people who have shared life over a long period are more likely to find their relationships and their obligations more significant than those who chance to meet in a brief encounter.

• *The commitment which each person makes to the other and the trust which each person has in the other.* People make promises to one another. Those promises become crucial in shaping their lives together and their expectations of each other. The meaning of giving appropriate priority to each other in that situation is integrally involved with the commitments which they have accepted freely.

• *The range of the relationship influences the obligation of loyalty.* A salesperson in a store and a customer have limited interests. The one wants to make a sale; the other wants to buy.

• *The "space" for the relationship.* There are many occasions when we would like to get to know people better, when we would like to understand them and share with them something of ourselves. But there are too many other persons demanding our attention. There are too many other loyalties which have legitimate claim on us to permit our concern for that person to be expressed in extensive ways.

• *The role of each person in the relationship.* Parents have different kinds of loyalty toward their own children than they do toward all other children. Gordon Kaufman has described the situation accurately.

As a father I have particular obligations to my own children which I do not have to others: I am charged in a special way with their care and upbringing. As a son I have particular obligations to my parents which I do not have with respect to other adults. As a teacher I have a special responsibility for my students which I do not have for everyone I meet on the street. If I were a doctor, I would have particular responsibilities to the sick; if a newspaper editor, to my readers; if a merchant, to those who bought from me. We always play definite roles in the various communities in which we participate, and these roles lay upon us special responsibilities which we are obligated to discharge.[1]

• *The "chemistry" of the relationship.* Some people get along with each other; some people just do not have rapport with each other. A relationship takes on profound meaning when two persons share easily their thoughts, longings, hopes, dreams, fears, hurts, successes. When persons have shared freely and deeply with each other, their loyalty to one another takes on significant dimensions not found in the contact between those who do not find it possible to share so openly.

In such varied situations, how do we manifest a primary concern for persons by our loyalty? Although the way in which our loyalty to the other gets expressed does vary with the meaning of our relationship, there are certain fundamental characteristics of loyalty which can be discerned whatever the situation.

First, to be loyal to others is to be faithful to the promises we have made to them. The promise may be simply an agreement to meet at the corner of Main and Oak at two o'clock in order to have a cup of coffee together, or the promise may be the marriage vow to love and to cherish until death. The impact of violating these two vows would obviously be different on the persons involved. In both cases, however, genuine concern for the person will mean keeping the promise. A promise is a pledge that we will do something in the future. Our relationship with others is enhanced, and we affirm to them that we take them seriously, when we honor the word which we have given.

Second, loyalty means fulfilling the obligations inherent in the situation in which we find ourselves. Obligations are respon-

---

[1]Gordon Kaufman, *The Context of Decision* Abingdon Press, 1961, p. 103.

sibilities we assume by virtue of offices we hold or roles we play. When a policeman directs traffic, he has an obligation to all drivers to keep things moving in such a way that cars do not run into each other. When a policeman holds his newborn daughter in his arms, he has a vast range of obligations toward that person.

The degree of our obligation will vary according to the nature of our involvement. But even in those relationships with minimal involvement it is appropriate to talk about obligation and loyalty. A clerk in the store may have no obligation to be concerned about the personal problems of the customer, but the clerk does have an obligation to help the customer find whatever he is looking for, to give prompt and efficient service, and to be accurate in describing the product being sold. The clerk also has an obligation to the employer to present the product as attractively as possible, to help the customer have a good attitude toward the store, and to be accurate in handling money. In this complex of obligations, the clerk truly expresses concern for persons by being loyal to his responsibilities toward those with whom he is dealing.

Third, loyalty means defending the interests and guarding the welfare of others. Genuine concern will lead us to keep faith with the other even when we have gone beyond any promises made or obligations accepted. When others have trusted us in such fashion that we are deeply involved in their welfare, loyalty means that we will stand by them whatever their need may be.

We cannot make unlimited commitments to everyone, for as finite persons we can be deeply involved with only a small group of persons. But there are those few with whom we do have limitless concern. Such loyalty, which exceeds any bounds of prudence or careful calculation, enriches human existence and is a demonstration of passionate concern for persons.

If we truly want to put persons first, we will demonstrate our priority by our loyalty to them in all of its various expressions and in all of our relationships—from the most casual to the most intense. However, it is not always easy to know what loyalty to others demands of us. Each of us stands at the center of a complex network of loyalties which we have to sort out carefully.

We may make promises in a burst of dedication which we cannot possibly keep for psychological, social, or physical reasons. Promises which lay claim on our loyalty need to be made with care. It may be devastating to another when we fail on our promise, though we have every will and intent to keep it.

We may be tempted to assume an obligation toward some persons which we do not have to take up, only to find that we are failing in our loyalty toward those who have a more appropriate claim on us. A father may spend all of his time as a Boy Scout leader to the almost total neglect of his relationship with his daughters.

Or we may find competing and conflicting claims of equal legitimacy and must make the painful decision of which loyalty we are going to affirm and which one deny. The clerk in the store may feel an obligation to tell the truth about a product to the customer. But she knows that it may cause her to lose her job, for her boss will be furious if she doesn't make this sale. Also she must consider her obligation to her mother who is dependent on her paycheck for food and rent.

. In many situations, when we try to assess the good we find ourselves weighing needs of persons which are in direct conflict. The thorny question of abortion, for example, is so difficult because we are confronted with the legitimate claim of persons to exercise control over their own lives and the equally legitimate claim of an unborn child to the right to life. Neither claim can be dismissed lightly if we are to put our priority on persons.

We do not deal adequately with a decision about abortion simply by invoking natural law or a civil law prohibiting such an action, as though the particular circumstance or need of the woman had no relevance to the decision. Neither do we deal adequately with the decision simply by declaring that people have a right to do with their bodies what they choose, as though the right to life of the unborn child was a frivolous matter.

To keep a gospel priority on persons calls us to be loyal to them. Also it will be helpful as we try to sort out the various claims made upon us, for often some of those competing claims are not intent on the good of people. But to keep a gospel priority on persons will not make our decisions simple or easy as we seek to live with loyalty in all of our relationships.

Loyalty to the Community

Our lives are involved not only with persons on an individual basis, but as members of a community. Reflecting on what it means to put persons first, we need to give consideration to ways in which our involvement in various communities assists or detracts from our expression of primary concern for persons. The term *community* is used here in a very broad sense, pointing to any group of persons who have some commonality which gives them a sense of identity and enables them to distinguish themselves from others

A brief look at some of the communities which make a claim on our loyalty will demonstrate the many ways in which our lives are tied up with persons in community.

• *Club or other voluntary groups.* People create all kinds of groups for all kinds of reasons. One of the most frequent comments people make when describing their town or city is that it is overorganized. People organize themselves to play bridge, to improve their schools, to discuss books, to provide insurance protection, to worship God, to beautify the city, to elect their own candidates to office, to make music, and so on.

• *Business or industry.* Relatively few people in our complex, technological society work alone. Most of us do our work in relation to a large number of other persons and perform specialized functions which are part of a larger process to which many persons contribute.

• *Town or city.* Towns or cities are political units which have responsibility for providing certain services for the people who live there. But for most of us the town is more than just the provider of services. It is important as a segment of our identity. It is the place of our belonging, the place where we are known, the place to which we return.

• *Nation.* Much of our life is shaped by the accident of our birth in a particular nation. How different life would be had we happened to have been born a citizen of China, or Zaire, or Finland, or Chile! It is the nation which protects us, which gives us citizenship, which demands our allegiance, which provides the symbols of flag and anthem.

• *Class.* Social class structure is a well-identified reality, even though class lines are imprecise and criteria for class identification are varied. Persons are identified with particular classes according to the amount of money they have or earn, the kind of job they hold, the kind and location of the house in which they live, the family of which they are a part, the amount of education they have, and the general style of their life. All of these factors are clearly important in the way persons live, and in determining with what other persons they will feel an identity.

• *Race.* We recognize that there are certain features about us which make us similar to some people and different from some people. People identify themselves with those with whom they share certain features, such as the color of the skin, or the shape of the head, or the texture of the hair.

• *Age.* Recently slogans have called attention to ways in which people relate to persons of their own age and feel themselves separated from those of a different age. There was talk of the generation gap, the demand never to trust anybody over thirty, or the Pepsi generation. People of certain ages do have interests in common, whether it be young people, or persons in mid-career, or retired people.

All of us thus find ourselves involved in many communities. We cluster together for many different reasons. We find a sense of oneness with others on many different grounds. As we reflect on how we express our concern for other persons, loyalty to the communities of which we are part becomes important.

When we voluntarily join a group, for whatever reason, we assume some obligations. As either employers or employees we have responsibilities toward others, and their welfare is dependent in part on what we do. To live in a town or city responsibly involves commitment to what we understand to be the best interests of that community and a willingness to work for those conditions which will bring the greatest opportunity of fulfillment for all the people. The nation can exist as a viable society only when its members demonstrate their loyalty to their country.

To recognize that we relate more easily to persons of the same class, race, or age is simply to acknowledge a fundamental reality in human existence. In every society persons tend to group themselves on the basis of factors which they share in common. Some of the most significant of these factors are the values and standards associated with class status, the marks by which racial discriminations are drawn, the interests associated with the age of a person. Human experience demonstrates repeatedly the power of such bonds in drawing people together in sustaining and cooperative endeavors.

The strength which comes when persons in groups are loyal to each other has made possible the achievements which have benefited those involved. The history of the labor-union movement, for example, demonstrates how a united strength can win conditions which make work more meaningful and fulfilling and can give dignity to people who were exploited as mere productive units when they were not bound together by a common loyalty. Emphasis on black power and solidarity has enabled many black persons to achieve a healthy sense of their own worth as they become aware of their particular heritage and struggle together to realize common goals. Young persons have found in their loyalty to each other the capacity to protest those values and actions in our common life which they see to be destructive. Older persons have found new dignity and meaning in their years as they have shared those concerns which are common to their age.

We have need for many kinds of communities. Our loyalty to those communities and our willingness to fulfill the obligations inherent in being part of them are a way of expressing concern, not only for our own need but also for the needs of others.

A Christian Perspective

Loyalty is one of the most cherished of human virtues. Philosophers have reflected on the importance of loyalty in all human relationships. Ethicists have pronounced loyalty to be one of the goods of life. Patriots have called for loyalty to flag and country as the prime obligation of all citizens. Educators have opened the school day by leading students in the pledge of allegiance. Family counselors have explored with persons the need for loyalty in this intimate relationship. Employers have championed the value of loyalty.

From many perspectives the significance of loyalty in human existence may be discerned. Thus the Christian faith can hardly claim this virtue as its exclusive insight. But there is a Christian perspective of this human virtue which can help us to perceive how it relates to the gospel priority on persons.

First, the Christian perspective reinforces the crucial importance of loyalty in human relationships. For example, Jesus cited this virtue as the distinctive mark of a "faithful and wise servant"

(Matt. 24:45-51). Such a servant, who was faithful to his trust, might expect to be set over all of his master's possessions. Failure to exercise his responsibilities, however, would result in a severe punishment.

In this illustration, the servant had an obligation to his master to care for the persons and the possessions which had been entrusted to him. Moreover, he had a responsibility to his fellow servants who were dependent on him while his master was away. The servant's role required a loyalty, to his master and to his fellow servants. Faithfulness to this trust would benefit not only the servant himself but also those whom he was charged to care for. A lack of faithfulness was disloyalty to the master and disaster to the servant.

Jesus called people to follow him, and he asked for loyalty of those who heeded his call. He gave of himself freely to those who became his disciples, teaching them, ministering to them, and entrusting his work to them. Because he had shared so fully and placed such trust in them, the Jesus' betrayal by Judas strikes us as a particularly heinous act and the failure of all the disciples to stay with their Lord as an unusually sad failure. This was no casual encounter between Jesus and his disciples but a deep and profound sharing. Their failure to be loyal to the one who had called them brought great suffering and destruction to them all.

Loyalty is not exclusively a Christian virtue, but the life and the teaching of Jesus testify that loyalty is an important dimension in creative and fulfilling human relationships.

Second, the Christian perspective breaks the exclusive character of many of our loyalties. So often loyalty to one person or to one group seems to mean that we must be opposed to other persons or other groups. This exclusive drive in loyalty is seen most often perhaps in our national life, where loyalty to our own country tends to get defined by the willingness to fight and even to destroy others. Even if patriotism is not defined solely in military terms, it then is defined in terms of our nation maintaining the economic and political strength to keep superiority over others. Or the values of pride, a sense of belonging, and an awareness of worth which come with loyalty to one's race are seriously compromised when loyalty to one's own race becomes equated with animosity to all other races. Even loyalty to the family can become narrow and self-centered, so that concern for the family isolates its members from involvement in the broader community.

It must be acknowledged that this narrow focus of loyalty has often characterized the religious community and been abetted by the religious conviction. To be loyal to the Christian religion meant that one had to be in vigorous opposition to all other religious traditions. Persistent efforts to convert the Jews or to resist the encroachment of the Buddhists are evidence of such a particularistic view of loyalty to one's own faith.

Within the Christian tradition itself, loyalty to one church has meant that there had to be separation from all other churches. To be a Catholic forced separation from heretical Protestants. To be a Protestant demanded condemnation of Roman papistry. To be a liberal Protestant carried an inevitable scorn for rigid evangelicals. To be an evangelical was to view liberal Protestants as persons who had sold out the heart of the faith.

Religious particularism has an inherent pressure toward a rigid and narrow meaning of loyalty, for religion deals with the most profound convictions by which persons live. It claims to articulate the truth. Loyalty to the truth has to take precedence over willingness to compromise in order to get along with people.

Even the biblical witness is ambiguous about whether loyalty demands an exclusive stance toward all others. When the people of Israel returned to their homeland from exile in Babylon, many of them had married persons of other nations and other religions. Ezra called the people together and condemned them in blunt language for their faithlessness. "You have trespassed and married foreign women, and so increased the guilt of Israel. Now then make confession to the LORD the God of your fathers, and do his will; separate yourselves from the peoples of the land and from the foreign wives" (Ezra 10:10-11).

The book of Ezra closes with a long list of names, followed by this sentence: "All these had married foreign women, and they put them away with their children" (10:44). What human anguish is involved in that brief, cryptic comment—women and children thrust away from husbands and fathers, homes broken, and people scattered.

Ezra was not a malicious destroyer of families but a man deeply concerned with what would happen to the identity of God's people if they did not guard themselves against the danger of simply becoming like the peoples around them. Loyalty to the people whom God had created meant that they had to isolate themselves from the corrupting influences of the folk around them, even if that isolation compelled them to drive husbands from their wives and fathers from their children.

Jesus too seemed at times ambiguous in his dealings with people outside his own heritage. There is the incident, for example, when a Greek woman, a Syrophoenician by race, begged him to cast the demon out of her daughter. "He said to her, 'Let the children first be fed, for it is not right to take the children's bread and throw it to the dogs' " (Mark 7:25-27).

These harsh words sound strange to us coming from the lips of Jesus. Can we interpret them as a literal statement of Jesus' atitude toward persons of a non-Jewish race? Was he simply repeating a popular expression to call attention to Jewish exclusiveness? Or should we assume, as some interpreters do, that this passage reflects a point of view attributed to Jesus by persons in the early church who sought to guard the purity of Jewish traditions by demanding obedience to the law?

However we may seek to interpret these words attributed to Jesus, we need to recognize that he did heal the woman's daughter. Moreover, we cannot forget that it was a Samaritan whom he chose to be the hero of one of his most memorable parables. (See Luke 10:29-37). As we view his total ministry, it is clear that loyalty to his own race did not exclude the condition of every person he met from his concern.

The biblical perspective which sees loyalty as able to accommodate an inclusive concern is not restricted to the New Testament. The rigid particularity of an Ezra is indeed part of the Israelite tradition, but so also is the story of Ruth, the woman of Moab. When Ruth's mother-in-law, Naomi, returned to her own land of Judah because of the death of her husband and her sons, she tried to persuade Ruth not to go with her.

There was nothing for Ruth to look forward to; Naomi had no other sons to offer. Ruth would be a stranger in a foreign land. But Ruth expressed her concern and compassion for her mother-in-law, who had been so bereaved, in the moving words: "Entreat me not to leave you or to return from following you; for where you go I will go, and where you lodge I will lodge; your people shall be my people, and your God my God; where you die I will die, and there will I be buried" (Ruth 1:16-17).

At the time when Ezra was driving husbands from their families, the story of Ruth dramatized how appropriate and right it was for loyalty to another person to transcend the loyalty to race and place and even religion. The story of Ruth concludes by noting that she became the great-grandmother of David, the king of Israel. In a quiet but sharp way the story aims at those who would be so rigid in the meaning of loyalty to Israel; it points out that the greatest king of all had a foreign ancestor.

Surely the biblical perspective helps us to see that loyalty to our own religion does not mean denigration of the faith of others. Moreover, loyalty to our own nation does not mean destruction of all others. Loyalty to our own race does not mean bitter animosity toward all others. Loyalty to our own family does not mean exclusive preoccupation with its needs. If persons are truly to come first, then those things which we use to give ourselves identity with a group must not raise barriers which keep us from awareness of the full humanity of any person.

Third, the Christian perspective sets our lives in the context of our ultimate loyalty to God and to him alone. Let us look at two implications of this assertion, one negative and one positive. To declare that our ultimate loyalty is to God is to affirm that there is nothing else which has that kind of claim on us. As we seek to live responsively to the gospel, we cannot give our final loyalty to nation, race, or to any institution of which we are a part. Neither our business nor our church is to be supported without equivocation under all circumstances.

To accept the Christian perspective that ultimate loyalty is owed only to God means that we cannot fulfill our responsibility in every situation simply by responding to the claim which any institution or any person makes upon us. We cannot solve the problem of how we ought to live with others by always being a loyal citizen, by always being a devoted parent, by always putting our business first, by always making every effort to defend our family. To put ultimate loyalty in God means that ultimate loyalty can be put in no other person or institution.

To put our ultimate loyalty in God has a positive meaning for us. It means that the will of God will be sought in every circumstance. However, this poses the difficult question of what the will of God is and how it can be discerned. We do not always get a clear mandate from God. In facing tough moral decisions, we find ourselves weighing conflicting values and struggling with competing claims. Nevertheless, we are not left without guidance.

To put our ultimate loyalty in God is to seek to order our relationships with others in the spirit of Jesus Christ. As we noted in the first chapter, Jesus does not provide principles which will cover every decision nor offer us an example to guide us in every circumstance. But he does embody the purpose of God.

It is significant for us to ask whether the decisions we are making and the relationships we are establishing are appropriate to the kind of life to which we believe Jesus Christ leads us. As we seek to discern the will of God for us, the entire biblical witness bears testimony to who God is and what his ways are in our world. The Bible may not provide ready answers to tough problems, but it does set the direction in which God's purposes are moving.

Ultimate loyalty to God will also serve to enable us to deal with the claims of lesser loyalties. Two examples will suffice to make the point clear. Jesus invited persons to follow him in these terms: "If any man would come after me, let him deny himself and take up his cross and follow me" (Mark 8:34). We are always tempted to give our first loyalty to ourselves, to do those things which will benefit to us personally. Our Christian commitment does not turn us automatically into selfless beings, but it does set before us the constant claim that we have a higher obligation. We are called to deny ourselves and to give our allegiance to Jesus Christ.

Peter and John provide the other example. They were arrested in the temple at Jerusalem for healing in the name of Christ, and declaring his resurrection. After due consideration, the elders and scribes warned them to speak no more of him. "But Peter and John answered them, 'Whether it is right in the sight of God to listen to you rather than to God, you must judge; for we cannot but speak of what we have seen and heard' " (Acts 4:19-20). Loyalty to God enabled these two men to resist the pressures of the authorities and enabled them to persevere in the witness which they believed to be true.

Fourth, the Christian perspective enables us to discern the meaning of loyalty from within the Christian community. Our ultimate loyalty is not to the church as an institution. We are not called as Christians to defend the church against all critics or to give priority to the church over all other institutions. But we are part of a community in which people do seek to be responsible to each other in the spirit of Christ.

In the church we have some experience of what human loyalty can mean as persons demonstrate a concern and compassion for one another. Out of our life in the fellowship of Christ's body, loyalty can be a living reality rather than an abstract concept.

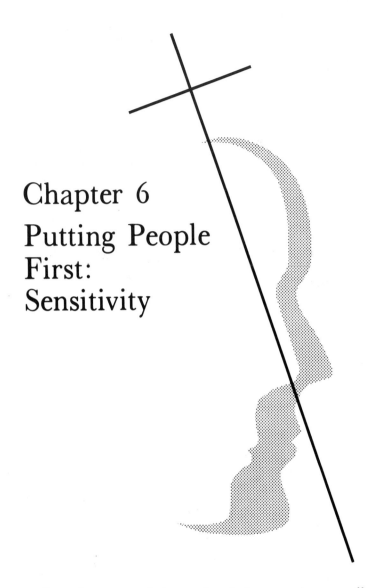

Chapter 6
Putting People First:
Sensitivity

Commitment to the gospel priority on persons calls for cultivating a sensitivity to individuals in order that we may be genuinely responsive to them. Unlike a machine, for example, a person is not an object to be manipulated according to our own whims. Persons are subjects, not objects. If we genuinely care about others, if we are truly concerned for persons, we need to be sensitive to what is happening in their lives.

Being sensitive to others is no easy accomplishment. Each one is an individual. Every person is infinitely complex and subtle. We can never fully know another person, even one with whom we may live for many years. However, sensitivity can be developed if we care about persons.

In this chapter, we seek to understand a bit more fully what it means for us to express our priority on persons by trying to be sensitive to them.

Our Perception of Persons

None of us, at any given moment, has a total perception of every object or sound within the range of our eyes and ears. The nervous system simply could not bear the impact. No matter how familiar a particular scene may be, we can always see something in it that we have not seen before if we look intently. Our ears are constantly bombarded by sounds, but we usually hear only those to which we pay attention. We have to be selective about what we see and hear; in order to focus attention on one thing, we need to shut out a host of other sights and sounds.

Even when we look and listen it is not always easy to see or to hear. A person with a trained eye will see far more in a fine painting, for example, than a person who is not familiar with art. A mechanic can often tell a good deal about what is going on under the hood of a car simply by listening to the engine. Such skills require cultivation.

When we are in the presence of another person, the difficulty of seeing and hearing makes great demands on us. There are so many things going on inside every person we meet—a wide range of feelings and thoughts, of hopes and fears, of longings and frustrations. How can we possibly perceive all that another person is thinking and feeling?

Persons communicate in many ways. In order to see and hear another, many kinds of signals must be read and interpreted. There are verbal signals, of course, but words must be listened to carefully and interpreted. People do not always say exactly what they mean, and they may even use words to cover up what is happening inside themselves. In many nonverbal ways persons give clues which can give us some insight into their thoughts and feelings: their facial expression, the way they hold their arms, the manner of their walk, the tense or relaxed state of their bodies, the expression in their eyes.

If we are going to put people first, somehow we have to learn how to see and to hear persons. As we try to understand what the gospel priority on persons means in our daily relationships, the way in which Jesus approached people is helpful to us. The Gospels mention occasions when Jesus performed miracles of healing at a distance, provided bread for large crowds, and taught the multitudes. But most of the impact of Jesus on people came through significant personal relationships with them, relationships informed by his sensitive perception of their situations.

There is repeated and impressive testimony in the Gospels to the way Jesus could see people. When a group of men carried a paralytic into his presence, Jesus saw their faith and offered forgiveness of sins. When the crowds followed him, he was sensitive to their hunger. When scribes questioned among themselves, "Jesus, knowing their thoughts, said, 'Why do you think evil in your hearts?'" (Matt. 9:4). A woman in a crowd touched him in order to be healed, and Jesus sensed the power which passed between them. Jesus was quite aware of the strengths and the weakness of Peter, and of the other disciples.

To Jesus people were not simply objects to be saved or bodies to be fed or sick organisms to be healed. They were persons, to be heard and responded to. The Gospel of John is particularly aware of Jesus' capacity to perceive what was going on in other persons, a capacity described explicitly when John wrote that Jesus "knew all men and needed no one to bear witness of man; for he himself knew what was in man" (John 2:25).

Perhaps the most significant thing we communicate to persons, when we take the time and effort really to see them, is that we think they are important. Simply listening and really hearing what another is saying affirms that we care. People need to have the experience of being understood. How often there are cries of loneliness and anguish which plead for a relationship in which someone understands: "You didn't listen to me." "Nobody knows what I am going through." "Why doesn't anybody pay any attention to me?" "Nobody understands me."

Sharing the problems of another person does not mean that we have quick and easy solutions to offer. The sharing in and of itself is important. But if we are to be helpful to persons in working out their problems, there must be honest insight into what their situation actually is. Sympathy with what a parent is suffering when a child dies may enable us to offer a presence or even a word of comfort and strength. Reacting to the wrong another person has done the possibility of being creative when we have some insight into who that person is.

Sensitivity to what it means to be constantly frustrated and deprived can help us to know what the poor in our society must endure. It may enable us to seek ways to help them while protecting their dignity and sense of worth. Awareness of other persons' situations will help us make judgments about them which are appropriate and meaningful.

Just as some people have a greater capacity to appreciate a painting or a piece of music, so some people have greater perceptiveness when they deal with other persons. But the ability to appreciate a painting or a symphony is disciplined and developed, and whatever our capacity for knowing other persons, we can develop our sensitivity. To see and to hear others requires that we make the effort to look and to listen.

To appreciate requires empathy, the capacity to put ourselves in the place of others. It requires imagination to know how others must be feeling in the situations in which they find themselves. Empathy and imagination can be nurtured so that we can share in part what other persons are experiencing.

An incident in the life of King David illustrates the significance of having the imagination which enables us to know what is happening to others if we are truly to be responsible in our relationships with them. With ruthless corruption, David trampled over the lives of other people. On one occasion he saw a woman bathing, and sent servants to command that Bathsheba come to him. When she became pregnant he sent for Uriah, her husband, who was a soldier in the king's army. Uriah returned from the battlefield but refused to go to his wife because the army was at war and men did not go to their wives at such a time. Even when David got him drunk, Uriah did not go to Bathsheba. So David sent him back to the army with instructions to Joab the commander to put Uriah at the forefront of the hardest fighting and then to leave him exposed so he would be killed. Joab did as he was instructed and in the fighting some of the servants of David were also killed. After Bathsheba mourned for her husband, David took her in and made her his wife.

David probably found the incident a bit unpleasant. He had to go to some trouble to make it appear that Uriah was the father of the child. He lost some of his servants in the process. But David did not appear to be too upset by the whole affair. He took Bathsheba in, made her his wife, and life settled down.

Then the prophet Nathan showed up to confront King David. But Nathan did not blast David for what he had done. Instead he told the king a simple story about a rich man who had many flocks and herds and a poor man who had only one little ewe lamb. When the rich man had a guest, he did not want to use his own sheep, so he took the poor man's one lamb and ate it. David got very angry and vowed that the rich man would restore the poor man's lamb fourfold. Then the prophet hit him: "You are the man." David saw what he had done and cried out: "I have sinned againt the Lord" (1 Sam. 12:13).

The prophet had stirred David's imagination until he realized what he had done to other people. As long as David was satisfying his own lust or trying to get himself out of a ticklish situation, he did not realize or care about what he was doing to others. David did not lack a capacity for moral indignation. He got very upset about the prophet's story of a rich man who took the one precious possession of a poor man. But until the prophet stimulated his imagination, David failed to perceive what his own actions meant in the lives of others.

Unless we develop our capacity to enter into the lives of others, we fail in our responsibility toward them. Until we can perceive, at least in part, what others are thinking and feeling, we will not know the impact of our actions, nor what their needs really are. To put persons first is to look and to listen with imagination.

Penitence for Wrongdoing

To be sensitive to persons is to be penitent for any wrongs involved in our relationships with them. Again the example of David illustrates how a concern for what is happening to others leads to penitence, and how penitence changes the character of a relationship. When David started caring about people, he repented of what he had done.

David's penitence brought a profound change in himself. He could not give back to Bathsheba her innocence. He could not give back to Uriah his life. He could not stem the tragic results of his actions, as evidenced in the prophet's warning that the child was going to die. but David did show extraordinary concern for the child. He did sense the suffering of Bathsheba and went to her to comfort her. David's penitence marked a change from a hard, brutal, ruthless tyrant to a sensitive, suffering, compassionate human being.

When we have hurt or wronged another, several things can happen. We may simply go on as though no wrong has been done—either because we are unaware of what we have done, or because we do not care. We may be pleased because we have gotten some gain for ourselves at the expense of another. We may try to hide the wrong so that no one will find out about it. We may try to ensure that the other person cannot get back at us in any way. Or we may repent.

Of all the things that can happen when a relationship between persons has been torn by a wrong done, penitence is the most creative and responsible. When we are blind to the damage which we have done to others, we are likely to continue trampling on those who get in our way. There can be no healthy contact between us and the other person when there is such fear of what we will do. When we arrogantly use our strength deliberately to gain personal advantage at the expense of another person, there can be no trust and confidence between us. When we have no regret for the harm we have done, we can not accept the forgiveness which may be offered. When we persist in separating ourselves from others, we build barriers against the healing and forgiving love of God in our own lives.

The crucial character of penitence for each of us personally, and for our relationships with others, is underscored by Jesus as he began his ministry with the announcement: "The time is fulfilled, and the kingdom of God is at hand; repent, and believe in the gospel" (Mark 1:14). To see life in the perspective of its fulfillment in Jesus Christ, and to live in the expectation of the rule of God in his world, is to be made aware of the corruptions in our lives, and the distortions which have fouled our dealings with others. Jesus announced his own coming as the breaking in of that sovereign power of God. In the presence of that new reality the response called for is penitence.

In Jesus Christ we know how we have failed others who depended on us and how we need to be open to the creative and healing love of God. When the priority of persons becomes the central concern of our lives, our need to restore broken relationships with others constrains us to seek them out with penitence. Sensitivity to who we are and what we have done to others confirms that the word of Jesus is addressed to us: "I have not come to call the righteous, but sinners to repentance" (Luke 5.32). Penitence opens our lives to the healing of God's forgiveness. In the dynamics of human relationships, something profound can happen when we have the sensitivity to be sorry for the hurt done and the grace to express our regret.

Penitence is a complex of attitude and action. First, it involves our emotions and feelings. A penitent person is genuinely sorry for the wrong which has been done. There is anguish that the other person has been hurt. Therefore penitence means suffering. To refuse to recognize or acknowledge that we have done any wrong may spare us that suffering. But if we can hurt another person without feeling anything, we have lost a significant capacity to be human.

Second, penitence involves acknowledgement of the wrong done and the acceptance of responsibility for what has happened. If we feel sorry for what we have done but make no effort to reach out to the one who has been hurt, our feelings become maudlin sentimentality. Until we accept responsibility, penitence is frivolous and without serious significance.

Third, penitence means serious intent and effort to change the behavior which wrongs others. We may feel sorry that another has been wronged but still enjoy the gain which has come to us by virtue of our offense and know deep down that if the opportunity for such gain comes again we will probably take it. Or we may confuse the regret for the harm done another with the regret at getting caught. Serious penitence is an earnest desire to change the behavior which brings harm to another.

Finally, penitence means making whatever restitution is possible. It is more than saying, I'm sorry; it is doing all that can be done to alleviate the harm done. Penitence is an honest effort to restore the relationship which has been destroyed.

We do not find it easy to repent, with all that it means to be penitent. It is hard to acknowledge that we have been wrong. It is hard to reach out toward another person to apologize. It is hard to give up gains we have made at the expense of others, and to make restitution. It is hard to feel anguish at the sufferings we have caused. But concern for others which leads us to be sensitive will bring us to penitence.

Humility in Our Relationships

To be sensitive to persons is to be humble in our relationships with them. Awareness of wrongs we have done to them may lead us to humility, but humility is more than penitence and distinct from a sense of unworthiness because we have done wrong.

"He is a meek man." "She is a humble woman." It is not immediately evident that such descriptions are highly complimentary. To be a meek man or a humble woman is not what many people strive to achieve. In a listing of the dominant virtues exalted by our culture, meekness and humility would find themselves well down the list.

Meekness is often associated with weakness and timidity. It is the frail, fearful person who is meek in the presence of superiors. The meek one does not have the strength or the determination to deal forcefully with others. When persons lack confidence in their own ideas and abilities, they bow meekly before the aggressive leadership of others.

Humility is often associated with inadequacy. There is the quick, snide dismissal of one who describes himself as humble: "Well, he's got a lot to be humble about." It is the failures of this world who are humble. People who do not have anything to be proud about are the humble, because they have no other option. Humble persons lack conviction about their own worth.

Because meekness and humility are not the most characteristic virtues of our culture, the words of Jesus in the Sermon on the Mount have an odd ring about them. "Blessed are the poor in spirit. . . .Blessed are the meek" (Matt. 5:3, 5). We may dismiss the notion that Jesus affirmed the blessedness of a pallid weakness, a destructive self-loathing, a bumbling failure. When these words spoken by Jesus are heard in the context of his life, we gain insight into what qualities of life he was affirming.

In Jesus' own life there is vivid expression of humility and meekness, but the words "weak" and "inadequate" are hardly the adjectives appropriate for him. It will help to sharpen the meaning of Jesus' words to note that the opposite of humble is not adequate. We do not speak accurately when we contrast humility and adequacy. Rather, the opposite of humble is proud. The opposite of meek is not strong, but arrogant.

The concern is whether proud arrogance or humble meekness lead to creative human relationships. The gospel priority on persons is best expressed when there is the sensitivity to others which comes with humility and meekness. There is blessing to the poor in spirit and the meek, and blessing through them to others.

A proud arrogance disrupts relationships; a humble meekness creates the possibility of genuine sharing between people. How the arrogant spirit disrupts the interaction between persons is illustrated in the incident when James and John came to Jesus to ask a favor. When Jesus inquired what they wanted, they indicated that they wanted to sit on his right hand and his left hand in his glory. Jesus responded that such places of glory were not his to give.

But the incident did not end with Jesus' conversation with the two brothers. The rest of the disciples got into it. "When the ten heard it, they began to be indignant at James and John" (Mark 10:41). They were indignant because they resented the bold arrogance of James and John in asking for such places of honor, and they were fearful that maybe they were going to miss out if they let someone else get ahead of them. Jesus had to take the time to deal with the animosity which was troubling the whole group of his disciples.

To approach other persons with arrogant demands or a proud sense of superiority threatens them. When people are threatened they react with fear or hate or aggressiveness. When we push our demands, the other person is only challenged to push his demands. When we assert our superiority, the other must either make his own claim or accept the inferior status to which we have assigned him. To come at others with humility and meekness enables them to respond to us without having to assert their own claims or to defend their own status.

A proud arrogance makes demands; a humble meekness enables service. In dealing with the tensions felt by his disciples because of the request of James and John, Jesus put the whole incident in a broader perspective.

> He said to them, "You know that those who are supposed to rule over the Gentiles lord it over them, and their great men exercise authority over them. But it shall not be so among you; but whoever would be first among you must be slave of all."
> —Mark 10:42-44.

There are many needs of persons to which we can minister if we are not desperately concerned to get all we can for ourselves. The willingness to do whatever needs to be done for another may not lead to glory and authority, but it will enable us to use the resources God has given to us for the blessing of others.

In our time, we have heard cries for power and for self-determination. Surely it is a legitimate effort for oppressed people to struggle for the right to shape their own destiny, whether they are oppressed because of poverty, race, or sex. The poor rightly demand that the total resources of a society be so used that all people have the dignity and integrity of providing for themselves. Black power advocates have made it clear that black people do not want to be cared for, but want the opportunity to care for themselves. Women who struggle against the sexism in our society make the valid point that it is destructive for persons to be denied positions of authority, opportunity for advancement, and equal pay because of their sex.

Those of us who have power and those of us who seek power both face the issue of whether we are going to use our power with a proud arrogance or a humble meekness. To be totally dependent on the beneficence of others is degrading; to be completely indifferent to the needs of others is destructive. To be forced to be servants of others is demeaning; to be freely servants of others is creative. The humility to serve others with our power enables us to use our power both for the blessing of ourselves and the other.

A proud arrogance focuses on ourselves; a humble meekness enables us to be aware of others. If we do not always have to be concerned about our status and our rights, we can give attention to what is happening to others. If we do not have to get credit for the good we do, there is no limit to the help we can offer.

There can be an awesome strength in the humble who do not have to worry so much about themselves, the strength of those who can give full attention to realization of the values they hold. It is the meek who have the strength to suffer in witness to the truth rather than making others suffer to further their own cause. It is the humble who can be sensitive to others.

As was suggested earlier, humility and meekness are not the prime virtues of our culture. Part of the reason is the notion that humility and meekness mean inadequacy and weakness. But even a more significant understanding of these qualities of life will not commend them to many. For we live in a culture which defines successful people as those who know how to achieve their own goals. They are the people who can move into any situation with a confident aggressiveness. They are the people who are looked up to and exalted. They are the people who win the struggles, who get what they desire, who make others do what they want.

If we take seriously the gospel priority on persons, the humility asked of us will not come easily. The pressures of the world around us set another style. We will not become the meek by easy acceptance of established ways but only by a determined response to the claim of Jesus Christ who said of himself: "For the Son of man also came not to be served but to serve, and to give his life as a ransom for many" (Mark 10:45).

Openness to Receive

To be sensitive to persons is to have the openness to receive what they can offer to us.

A disgruntled parishioner once complained that the church was always asking people to give. The response to his complaint was that "give" is a superb definition of the Christian life. Repeatedly Jesus called people to leave what they had and follow him, to give away their possessions to the poor. His life and teaching cut vigorously across the passion to get. When we are aware of the hurts and needs of others, such sensitivity calls us to give.

Sensitivity to and concern for others will also make it possible for us to receive what they have to give. Jesus exhorted people to give, he pushed them to give, he challenged them to give. He gave of himself without reserve, even to the limit of his life. But Jesus was also ready to receive from others.

One dramatic moment will serve to illustrate Jesus' awareness that people needed to be able to do something for him. He was at Bethany in the home of Simon the leper. A woman came with a jar of expensive ointment and proceeded to put it on Jesus' head. The disciples thought that was a waste because the ointment could have been sold and the money given to the poor. But Jesus saw what it meant for the woman to be able to do something for him. He saw her need to express her love by an extravagant and "useless" act. So he rebuked his disciples. "Why do you trouble the woman? For she has done a beautiful thing to me" (Matt. 26:10).

Usually we tend to think of giving as one of the more difficult forms of expressing concern for persons. Surely it would be easier to receive than to give. But, in fact, many of us find it quite difficult to accept a gift or offer of help from another person. This is vividly illustrated in one account of Jesus' last supper with his disciples.

In the Fourth Gospel we read that, following their final meal together, Jesus took a towel and a basin of water and began to wash the feet of his disciples. At least one of the disciples was not quite prepared to accept this gracious act of hospitality.

> He came to Simon Peter; and Peter said to him, "Lord, do you wash my feet?" Jesus answered him, "What I am doing you do not know now, but afterward you will understand." Peter said to him, "You shall never wash my feet."
> —John 13:6-8.

It is not difficult to understand Peter's initial reaction. By washing the feet of his disciples, Jesus exposed their foolish pride which had kept all of them from performing this service for one another and that was a bit embarrassing. If they let the Master wash their feet, there would be no service too humble for the disciples to offer others, and that was more than a bit threatening. So Peter resisted until Jesus insisted that he must do this for him.

It was as important for Peter to receive as it was for him to be committed to giving.

There is something destructive in a relationship when a person is always seeking to get something from others. But to be always giving can be as destructive as to be always getting. To be the one who always gives can be a way of trying to manipulate and control the other. Persons who always give want others to be dependent on them, or to be grateful to them, or to do what they want because they are obligated to them.

If we always have to give, there is a blatant refusal to acknowledge the contribution which other persons can make to us. It is a flagrant "put-down" when what persons have to give is rejected, as though they did not have anything significant to contribute to a relationship. Never to receive from others is one way of saying that they are really not very important and denies to them the joy of being needed.

If there is a grace in knowing how to give, there is also a grace in knowing how to receive. It is evidence of our concern for others when we have the sensitivity to receive those things they can give and to accept those things they can do.

Honesty in Our Dealings

To be sensitive to persons is to be honest with them. There is a significant difference between commitment to honesty as a principle and commitment to honesty as an expression of our concern for persons. To be committed to honesty as a principle simplifies life. We simply speak the truth as we see it regardless of the consequences to ourselves and others.

Commitment to honesty as a principle means telling the whole truth in every circumstance. There is much to be said for exalting honesty as a principle, because there are always temptations to avoid telling the truth, there are always rationalizations which can justify not speaking the truth.

Yet there is risk even in a commitment to honesty as a principle, as there is risk of distortion in every human circumstance. Commitment to truth can become a dogmatic arrogance, and we may confuse speaking the truth as we see it with speaking the truth. Determination to speak honestly can become an excuse for abusing and cutting down other people. To always "tell it like it is" may simply be our way of trying to coerce people into doing what we want. Speaking the truth may be done without regard for persons and what happens to them as a result of our speaking.

Commitment to honesty as an expression of our concern for persons is a different kind of commitment. It too has its risks. We may use a supposed concern for persons as a way of escaping the hard demands for truth-telling. The integrity of the demand for truth will be lost if we find ourselves justifying blatant dishonesty, or telling less than the whole truth on the ground that the good of the other person demands that we distort or conceal the real situation. Escaping the demand for honesty because we are concerned about persons may be our way of trying to dominate persons by doing what we think is best for them and not respecting their right to make their own decision on the basis of a full evaluation of the facts.

Often it is hard to be honest. Often it is painful to make ourselves aware of the truth. Often it is difficult to speak the truth. What problems do you see in responding to situations such as the following?

• A teacher talks with a student who is thinking of applying for graduate school, and who earnestly wants preparation for the career she has chosen. The teacher likes the student but has some serious reservation about her ability to do the work. The teacher also knows that the student will be terribly upset if she is discouraged from following her plans.

• After talking with the doctor and learning that his wife has cancer which will probably kill her within one or two months a man goes into the hospital room to face his wife's questions about her condition.

• A wife learns that her husband is having an affair with her best friend, but when she goes to a family counseling service she is rather nonchalant about the whole thing, even asserting that she really does not mind the situation.

• A person asks his friend's opinion about an article which he has purchased. The friend really does not like it but knows that the other person is just asking his opinion so he can hear someone praise his purchase.

• A candidate is meeting with the committee to select a new minister for the church. When asked about her views on certain social issues, she knows that if she expresses her real opinion there will be some members of the committee who will disagree sharply and who may be quite offended.

Such examples illustrate some of the difficulty and pain involved in facing and speaking the truth. We may shrink from making honest statements because we find the truth too difficult to deal with ourselves, and we prefer to keep it unexpressed. Or we may decide that the other person is not able to hear and to deal with the truth. Fear of offending others may cause us to be less than totally honest, or we have certain worthy goals in mind which appear to us to be in jeopardy if the full truth is spoken.

Genuine concern for persons and sensitivity to their situations will press us toward honesty, for we are really not taking the other person seriously if we use a supposed concern for them to escape the hard truths. But we seek honesty not simply for its own sake alone, but for the sake of persons.

The apostle Paul put the way of truth-speaking clearly when he wrote to the Ephesians that "speaking the truth in love, we are to grow up in every way into him who is the head, into Christ" (Eph. 4:15). A bit later he wrote: "Therefore, putting away falsehood, let every one speak the truth with his neighbor, for we are members one of another" (vs. 25). Truth spoken in love is our commitment to honesty as an expression of our concern for persons.

To speak the truth in love is creative of relationships between persons. Only when we are honest with each other can others count on what we say, or can we depend on what others say. When persons care for each other, they will risk the pain of honest reproof. When persons will risk being honest, they can share deeply their thoughts, feelings, and needs.

When we put persons first we are concerned about not hurting them, or about being nice to them. But not hurting others and being nice to others is not the same thing as loving others. Speaking the truth in love will be done, even if it is painful and offensive, when honest speaking is necessary for the welfare of others.

There must be sensitivity about when and how the truth is to be spoken if our priority is on persons. Speaking the word of truth is not done in isolation, but in a total context of love and care. We may not be able to speak some truth to some individuals because the fabric of our relationship will not enable the truth to be affirmed or heard. When we speak the truth, we must test our own spirit to discern as best we can that our honesty expresses profound concern for the welfare of the other.

When we refrain from speaking the truth, we must also test our own spirit. When it seems to us that the welfare of the other person calls for something less than total honesty, it may be our own fear or cowardice which keeps us quiet. For example, the teacher talking with the student about graduate school may shrink from honest appraisal because of a personal desire to avoid an unpleasant scene. Real concern for the student would compel an honest assessment so that the student does not proceed blindly to a decision which may waste great resources of time and money.

The family of a dying patient may think they are trying to spare the patient by refusing to speak of the coming death, when actually they fear to speak because, understandably, they are having trouble handling the reality of death themselves. Yet those who have experience in dealing with dying persons find that so often honest speaking with each other helps all concerned to face what is coming more creatively and courageously.

Putting people first means to be sensitive to them. We need to cultivate a sensitivity that enables us to see them and hear them, a sensitivity that helps us to relate to them with penitence and humility, a sensitivity that makes us open to receiving what they can offer to us, and a sensitivity that provides the possibility of honest speaking with love. Responsible relationships with others are complex and subtle affairs, demanding all of the creative effort we can give.

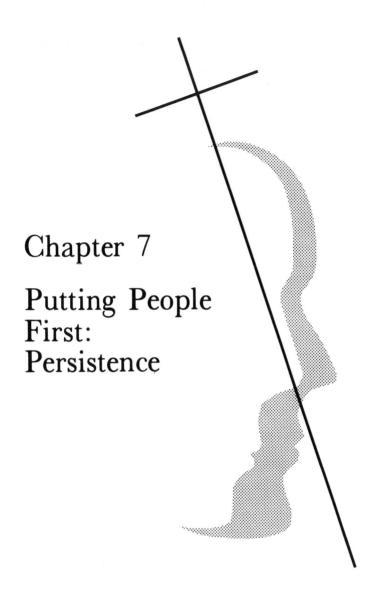

Chapter 7

Putting People First: Persistence

Anyone who works with people encounters many problems. A bus driver can recount endless tales about the people he has to deal with. A marriage counselor is exposed to countless ways people abuse each other. A store clerk, a union organizer, a foreman, a social worker, a minister, a school teacher, a lawyer, an umpire—all these will testify that people can be difficult.

Ways people can be objectionable are many and astounding. They can be surly, snappish, and quick to make nasty comments. With great ingenuity, they can find ways to keep from doing the jobs which are legitimately their responsibilities. They repeatedly make the same mistakes. They rebel against proper authority and refuse to cooperate with those trying to get a job done. In every possible way they take advantage of others. They are unreasonable in their complaints and with great vigor berate anyone who makes a mistake. They take delight in spreading malicious gossip and are quick to make fun of the limitations of others. When they cannot have their own way, they sulk and get moody. They have weird and offensive habits and are thoughtless of the feelings and needs of others.

When we set out to put priority on persons, we need to be aware of what we are getting into and to understand that we are going to run into problems. People are just not always going to listen to the sound advice we give them. Often they have little intention of changing their behavior or their attitudes. If we try to be helpful, they may take advantage of our generosity. Gratitude may be one of the virtues notably lacking, so that our efforts are met with a dismal lack of appreciation.

If we are sincere when we make our commitment to the gospel priority on persons, it will demand of us a willingness to persist. Some of the ways in which persistence needs to be expressed will be explored in this chapter.

Persisting in Patience

If we care for persons, we must persist in being patient with them. It does not require much effort on our part to get so angry with people that we cut off all communication with them. It does not require much devotion on our part to get so disgusted with people that we gladly get rid of them. Hurling thunderbolts of judgment at people for their many failures may be satisfying for the hurler, but it usually does little good for the one at whom they are aimed. Putting persons first calls for patient persistence in putting up with their perversities.

Patience often gets identified with passivity. If we are patient, it means that we are not going to do anything precipitously, which then gets translated into meaning that we are not going to do anything. To be patient with people then is simply to put up with them, to endure them, to hang on no matter what they do. If we seek from the biblical witness an understanding of what it means to be patient with people, it turns out to be considerably less passive than we often make it.

Jesus' persistence with his disciples serves as one illustration. He gathered this group of men about him, calling them from their work to follow him, and sending them out to preach and to heal in his name. With an eager enthusiasm the disciples followed him, sharing his life and his ministry. But again and again the disciples failed him—they did not understand what he was talking about, as they showed how little faith they had, as they missed the whole point by being more concerned with seats of honor than with places of service, as they ran in fear when the authorities closed in on Jesus.

Jesus never gave up on his disciples, not only because he wanted them to carry on his work, but also because he had genuine concern for them as persons. With extraordinary patience Jesus taught them, rebuked them, commissioned them, trusted them, and never gave up on them.

Paul's treatment of the people he had gathered to be the church offers another illustration of the meaning of patience from a biblical perspective. Paul is not often thought of as a patient man in some meanings of the term. His relationships with his churches got a bit tense from time to time, particularly with the church at Corinth. He wrote them angry letters and they made nasty comments about him. Their morals were deplorable and their convictions questionable. Paul argued with them, chastized them, corrected them, rebuked them. But Paul never gave up caring about them, so that he could even write: "I have great confidence in you; I have great pride in you; I am filled with comfort. With all our affliction, I am overjoyed" (2 Cor. 7:4).

Paul did not let the present limitations of persons define his expectations of them. He did not let the littleness, bitterness, and hostility of others sour his life. He kept affirming the people, and expressing toward them the love which he had come to know in Jesus Christ. He was sensitive to every sign of the grace of God in the midst of their life. He looked with patient expectation for every expression of faith and love which could be discerned.

Dealing with people can be difficult. There are problems and tensions. People can be mighty unpleasant. But if we put people first, and if we are serious in seeking a creative relationship with them, we will persevere with patience.

To be patient is to look on our relationships with others as an opportunity rather than as a problem. Patience is not blind to the problems, but it keeps working on the potential for the good which God has instilled in every one of his creatures.

To be patient is to respect the differences in others and glory in the infinite mystery of the human personality. We run the risk, in our persistent efforts with others, of simply trying to make them be like us or do what we want them to do. We can be discouraged because other persons will not agree with us, but the purpose of reaching out to others is to enable them to fulfill their own lives not to make them like us. Patience accepts the differences of others, and rejoices in their gifts, their abilities, their uniqueness.

Finally, to be patient is to seek for the possibilities in a person at a particular time. We miss the possibilities of what can happen if we persist by defining patience as though we were just to wait until some future time when there were better possibilities and better people to work with. We often miss our opportunities with people because we are too busy getting ready for opportunities in the future—wait until the children are grown and then we can deal with them, wait until the boss retires and then we will have good relationships in the office, wait until the promotion comes and then there will be the opportunity to do something creative. To persist with patience is to seek steadily for those ways in which we can express our concern for persons now.

Persisting in Forgiveness

If we care for persons, we will persist in forgiving them. People are not only aesthetically offensive, crude, and objectionable, they can do profound harm to one another. A man spreads malicious rumors about a co-worker to have a better chance than the other person at a promotion. A woman has been entrusted by a retired couple to invest their modest savings, takes the money and leaves them almost penniless. A man tries to beat a red light and plows into the side of another car, killing a wife and mother of five children. A couple make clear in subtle but effective ways that they now find some former friends to be a bit beneath them. A husband constantly annoys his wife because he simply will not pick up the paper, hang up his clothes, or put his things away.

In our relationships with people, we too are sometimes wronged and harm is done to us. The hurt to us can range from minor irritation to serious injury, from a social offense to death of a loved one. What response can we make when we have been wronged? We have a number of options open to us as we deal with a person who has hurt us.

• *We can seek vengeance.* The other person hurt us, and we are going to find ways to get even. "An eye for an eye and a tooth for a tooth" is an ancient code in human history and many people still believe it is just. There seems to be a kind of justice in the notion that if a person has hurt us in some way he should suffer at least as much.

• *We can see that the offender is punished.* Persons must learn that it is wrong to do harm to others. One way that lesson can be effectively taught is to punish the person who has done the wrong. He must be made to suffer hurt, not for the satisfaction which comes to us when we get vengeance but for the good of the person that he will learn how to treat others responsibly.

• *We can insist that he be restrained.* If there seems to be danger of the person hurting others or hurting us again, we will try to find ways to remove the threat. One of the justifications of imprisonment is that those who have demonstrated by their past behavior that they are liable to do harm to others cannot be allowed to function freely in society.

• *We can try to forget the whole incident.* We can adopt the attitude that what's done is done, and that there is no point in continuing to worry about it. The best thing to do is to forget it and go on about the business of living.

• *We can seek restitution.* If there is some way in which recompense can be made for the damage done, we will insist that the person who has done the wrong be made to pay.

• *We can cut off all contact with him.* Because of what he has done to us, we find it very unpleasant to deal with him in any way, and so we will do everything possible to isolate ourselves from him.

• *We can forgive him and seek to be reconciled to him.* How we respond when we have been hurt will have a profound influence on the quality of our lives and of the other persons, and on the possibility of our future relationship with them. Not all the preceding options are mutually exclusive, of course. For example, we can insist that a dangerous person be restrained and either cut off all contact with him or maintain an on-going relationship. But of all the options noted, the gospel priority on persons leads us to forgiveness. To persist in our concern for persons means that we will forgive them when they have wronged us, for their welfare and for our own.

Many of us find it difficult to forgive. If a person accidently steps on our toe and apologizes profusely, we can be magnanimous and forgive him instead of trampling on his toe. But to forgive when someone has hurt us badly raises serious difficulties. It is possible that we can forgive when the damage has been serious or the offense prolonged? How can we forgive, for example, when the dreams of a lifetime have been shattered by the viciousness of another? How can we forgive the death of a loved one through the fault of another? How can we forgive when we have been abused and humiliated by another.

It seems almost instinctive for us to strike back, to find some way to get even. While not all the options noted are mutually exclusive, forgiveness and vengeance are. We simply cannot try to get even and forgive at the same time. In the struggle within us between desire for vengeance and the need for forgiveness, vengeance pulls strongly at us.

Imagine how we might respond in a situation like that in which Joseph finds himself in the biblical story. He had been sold into slavery by his brothers who were jealous of him. Years later, when Joseph is the second most powerful man in Egypt, his brothers stand helpless before him, and he can do with them anything he likes. A similar wrong done to us may lead us to fantasies about what we would do, given such an opportunity.

Many of us find it difficult to forgive because we rather enjoy the hatred for others which their wrong against us permits. There is a certain malicious delight in talking against them and reporting their abominable behavior to others. We rehearse to ourselves the wrong done to us and find our role as victim rather satisfying.

Then we can raise the question whether it is really proper to forgive. Is it appropriate to forgive a person when he has done serious wrong to us? If people are always forgiven for the wrongs they do, would that not be an open invitation to hurt others repeatedly for their own gain? How do we uphold standards of conduct if those who violate the standards are forgiven?

Joseph forgave his brothers as they stood frightened before him. (See Gen. 45:1-15.) Many of us may feel more in tune with Samson. The captors who had weakened him by cutting his hair and blinding him and throwing him in prison forget to keep his hair short. The day came when his captors brought Samson into the temple to torment him. Samson had a boy put his hands on the pillars of the temple and as he pulled on the pillars to bring the temple down, he cried out to God: "O Lord God, remember me, I pray thee, and strengthen me, I pray thee, only this once, O God, that I may be avenged upon the Philistines for one of my two eyes" (Judges 16:28).

How do we deal with our problems with forgiveness? Forgiveness will never be easy, but it was never promised to us that genuine caring for others would be easy. To persist in our concern for others even to the point of forgiving them when they have wronged us makes great demands on us and expresses a radical claim in the midst of a world more given to vengeance or punishment.

Two things may help us as we reflect on our own willingness and ability to express our concern for others by forgiving them: First, we need to understand what the meaning of forgiveness is in a Christian context. Second, we need to focus on what happens to people when they do or do not forgive.

Let us look at what it means to forgive. Many of us share with Peter the view that there ought to be some conditions connected with forgiveness. Peter heard Jesus calling people to forgive when they had been wronged. He decided that he would find out just what the conditions were under which forgiveness ought to be offered. "Lord, how often shall my brother sin against me, and I forgive him? As many as seven times?" Perhaps it would seem to us, as it did to Peter, that forgiving the same person seven times is going to considerable extreme.

Jesus had another view of forgiveness. There are no conditions, and in his response to Peter's question he makes that clear. "I do not say to you seven times but seventy times seven" (Matt. 18:21-22). If we are going to forgive, we forgive whatever the circumstances. If we are going to forgive, there are no conditions which have to satisfy us before forgiveness is offered.

The notion of no conditions for forgiveness poses considerable difficulty for us. We want to set some conditions. We will forgive if the offense is not too serious, or if it has not hurt us too badly. We will forgive if the other person will make proper restitution. We will forgive if we can be guaranteed that the offense will never happen again. We will forgive if the person is properly penitent. It does seem to us that the person we are forgiving ought to have the proper attitude if we are going to be so magnanimous.

In dealing with others, we are perfectly free to set the conditions for our forgiveness, of course. But let us not confuse that kind of forgiving with the forgiving of Jesus, with the forgiving of the gospel, with the forgiving to which the Christian calling commits us. When we persist with a gospel concern for others there are no limits and no conditions on our forgiveness.

Jesus also makes clear that forgiveness is not a passive refusal to strike back but an active seeking of good for the other. To forgive another is neither to condone the wrong that has been done nor to let the evil go unchecked. When Jesus dealt with the notion of an eye for an eye and a tooth for a tooth, he did not say simply that a person should not take revenge. Rather he called for reaching out with active goodwill and creative help to the other.

A slap on the right cheek, for example, is an insult, and if a person insults us, we turn the other cheek. This is a symbolic way of saying that we try to understand what need the person has which compels him to such offensive behavior and to respond to his need. If a person needs a coat badly enough to take it, he probably needs more help which we can offer. If a person has a burden he needs help in carrying one mile, we offer the help for the second mile. Jesus' forgiveness was not a passive acceptance of the evil people do but an active reaching out to touch their lives and to minister to them.

Then the biblical witness helps us to see what forgiveness means as it shows us the context in which we hear the admonition to forgive. We are not the righteous who magnanimously offer forgiveness to the unworthy sinner. We are the forgiven who are being asked to forgive. There is a different dynamic in our relationship with those who have hurt us in some way when we remember the forgiveness which has been granted to us by God and by our fellows.

Now, let us look at what forgiveness means in our own lives and in the lives of others. Forgiveness is an expression of the priority we place on persons. It represents a concern for the welfare of the person who has done the wrong. To forgive is to deal with the person, and not simply with the harmful act. Relationships between persons are obviously disrupted when damage is done to one person by another. Only forgiveness and reconciliation can reestablish that relationship with its potential for creative interchange.

We do have a number of options when an offense has been done against us. Vengeance is destructive, for it simply perpetuates and accelerates the breakdown between persons. Revenge invites its own retaliation. Punishment may be appropriate when it is so designed that it enables persons to learn appropriate behavior in dealing with others. But punishment without forgiveness becomes vindictive and reduces the possibility of real learning.

Restraint may be called for, for persons who do not have the capacity for responsible behavior in society must not be allowed to threaten all others. But restraint without forgiveness reduces the possibility of that healing which might enable the person to become responsible. Forgetting about what happened or isolating ourselves from the one who hurt us may seem to be the easiest solution. But it does not express our concern for the needs of the person who has done the wrong.

Forgiveness expresses the priority on persons, not only on others but also on ourselves. Only by forgiveness can we escape the terrible, destructive power of hatred in our own lives. To nurture bitterness against those who have done us wrong is to poison our own spirits. And forgiveness sets us free from having to deal only with the wrongs which have been perpetrated against us. There are so many richer things in life than avenging hurts.

Forgiveness is significant not only in personal relationships, but also in shaping the way society deals with those who commit offenses. A society has to protect its members against the assaults of those who commit criminal acts, and demonstrate its profound concern for those who are victims. But a healthy society also demonstrates profound concern for those who are guilty.

This concern is not readily manifest in our present penal system. Too many prisoners experience their incarceration as sheer vengeance and as unrestrained violence against their persons. The alarming rate of relapse into criminal behavior among previous offenders indicates that convicts find their prison experience is simply training for more effective crime and that society is not really prepared to accept them back. Sheer punishment without rehabilitation only embitters. Restraint with forgiveness only isolates.

The riots at Attica prison in New York State demonstrated tragically what can happen to persons in prison. Tom Wicker, who was a member of the negotiating committee at Attica was led to ask: "What are we doing caging people up like animals? Do we really believe that caging them will make better people out of them? The sheer, utter, incredible inhumanity of that place is so depressing. And the point is that Attica is *our* prison—*our* prison!"[1]

A gospel priority on persons compels us to be concerned not only about the physical and social conditions of our prisons, but also about what we as a society are seeking to accomplish when we imprison people. Our persistent concern for persons is manifest as we express forgiveness, both as individuals and as a society.

Persisting in Suffering

If we care for persons, we will persist even to suffering with them. Pain and suffering come to every person. Accidents will happen. Illness will come. Death is certain. The human body and the human spirit have marked sensitivity to pain.

There is one sure way to cut down the amount of suffering and to reduce the threats of suffering. There are many things persons will never suffer if they keep clear of all entanglements with others. If we refuse to get deeply involved with or decline to make any commitments to others, we will be spared much suffering.

---

[1] Quoted in *Wilderness Voices* by James Armstrong, Abingdon Press, 1974, p. 59.

But if we truly care for persons, we will persist even to suffering with them. The most profound implication of the gospel priority on persons is expressed in the central symbol of the Christian faith, the cross. Jesus died on a cross, a slow, anguished, tortured death. He did not have to die on that cross. He did not want to die on that cross. But he died on the cross, giving his life in sacrifice for others. The cross was only the last and the climatic event in Jesus' suffering for others.

Throughout all his ministry Jesus took upon himself the burdens, cares, and hurts of others. He suffered rejection by his own people. When he came to his own country, people refused to take him seriously or to hear what he had to say. He suffered because others were hurting, being moved by compassion when he saw the hunger or the illness of people. He suffered because of what he saw happening to his people, and because of the judgment he saw coming upon them. He went to Jerusalem knowing that there his enemies would seize him and kill him. As he entered the city he wept over it, crying out: "Would that even today you knew the things that make for peace" (Luke 19:43).

The life of Jesus was not a tragic disaster. It is not to be painted in somber, dark, and dreary tones. But throughout his life, Jesus suffered as he shared the hurts and took upon himself the pains of others. He suffered because he cared for people.

Jesus did not suffer and die to uphold an abstract principle of justice. He did not die in defense of a creedal statement. He did not die leading an armed revolt against the established power. Jesus was concerned about justice and beliefs. He was rightly perceived by the established authorities as a threat. But Jesus suffered because he shared deeply the needs and anguish of others. His death was a profound expression of his love for people, even those who crucified him. By his death for others Jesus took upon himself the burden of their sin, and through his death the forgiveness of God is offered with fresh conviction.

Through the death of Jesus God reached out to his people and restored a relationship with them which had been broken by their obstinate sin. Jesus' death on the cross is not a mechanical transaction by which the debts owed by persons are paid off. His death on the cross is his personal testimony of God's love for persons which comes with creative and transforming power.

Jesus did not have to suffer with others. He could have turned away from the sick and the hungry when he was tired. He could have given up on his own people and on his disciples when they showed how little faith and understanding they had. He could have turned his back on Jerusalem here men waited to crucify him. But Jesus did not turn away from his commitment to persons, even when the cost got frighteningly high.

A gospel priority on persons will lead us to persist in our concern for them even when that concern brings suffering. We don't have to care, but if we do care we become vulnerable. A friend weeps with a husband as he stands at the grave of his wife who was killed in a car accident. Parents share the anguish of their daughter whose husband suddenly deserts her and two small children. A fireman suffers severe burns because he goes back into the building to carry out a man trapped by the flames. A girl drowns as she jumps into the river to save her friends who had slipped off the bridge. A girl donates one of her kidneys to her sister. A person stands by a friend who is under attack even though it means his own job will be in jeopardy.

All of these people could have turned away. If a friend did not care, he would not weep with another at the grave of his wife. If a parent did not care, there would be no anguish when a daughter's marriage fails. If a fireman did not care, he would not go into a burning building to save another person. To put people first is to persist even to suffering.

Jesus could have turned away from the suffering and from the death. But what kind of man would Jesus have been and what kind of a God would he have witnessed to if he had grown hard against the poor and the sick, if he had fled in fear from his enemies in Jerusalem? His faithfulness to his commitment to persons even to suffering and death gives Jesus the stature which enables him to manifest both the fullness of God and the fullness of persons. For persons come to the full stature of what God intends them to be as there is a caring relationship with others, a caring relationship which involves the risk of pain, sorrow, suffering, and even death.

Thus to put people first demands persistence, a persistence which enables us to be patient when they are difficult, a persistence which expresses forgiveness when they have wronged us, a persistence which leads us to share their burden and their pain.

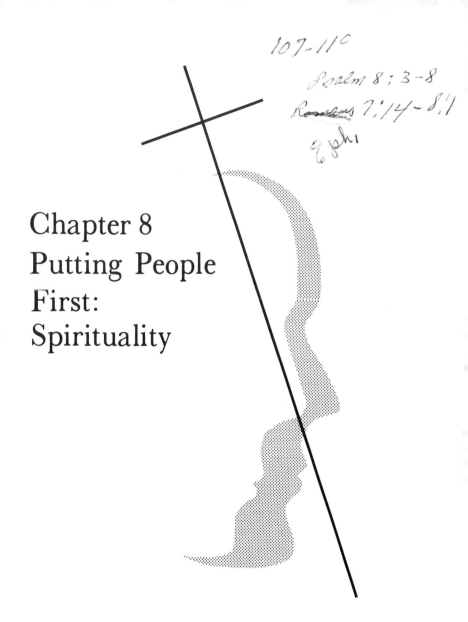

Psalm 8:3-8
Romans 7:14-8:1
Ephi

Chapter 8
Putting People
First:
Spirituality

Our priority on persons is demonstrated by a concern for their physical and psychological well being. The good is whatever brings health and wholeness to persons. But the gospel priority on persons does not let us stop with concern for their physical strength and psychological health.

The gospel leads us to ask what people are going to do with their strength and how they are going to use their health. When people have plenty to eat, a nice home, two cars, and adequate insurance the problems of life are not all solved. Profound concern for persons includes concern for the life of the spirit. Spirituality involves the health not only of the body or of the psyche but the health of the whole person.

Seeking God's Purpose

We return now to reflect directly on a question raised early on in our consideration. It was noted that there is general agreement on the priority of persons, that the plea to let people be human has become virtually a slogan. But what does it mean to be human? Any meaningful answer to that question involves convictions about who persons are and what purposes their lives are intended to fulfill. It touches upon the fundamental perceptions of reality and of self.

What does it mean then to be human? How do persons go about "making and keeping life human?" The question has been answered in a number of ways, for we are talking about the most significant commitments of life. To be human is to have the ability to determine our own destiny, is one answer. When the external and internal conditions of our lives allow us the freedom to choose what we are going to do, then we are genuinely and fully human.

Another answer is that to be human is to find self-fulfillment, to grow in our capacity to be in touch with our own selves and our world, to expand our consciousness and our awareness. It is the gratification of our desires and the expression of our "selves" which allows us to be fully human. Yet another answer is that to be human is to be happy. The more happiness we experience the more we realize the purpose for which our lives were given.

There are other ways we may talk about what it means to be human, of course, but these examples give some indication of the direction in which many persons look when they set out to define what the appropriate goals of human existence are. But we need to look at another kind of answer to the question of what it means to be human, an answer embodied in the person of Jesus of

Nazareth. The life of this man points us in a different direction as we look for the purposes which are worthy of the investment of life. For Jesus did not set out to fight for self-determination, nor to achieve expanded consciousness, nor to gain happiness.

Two things can be noted about the life of Jesus. First, his life was lived in response to the will of God and in a close relationship with God. There was always about him a sense of mission, an awareness that God had entrusted him with a ministry which called forth the best he had to give in body, mind, and spirit. The prime question of Jesus' life was not how he could find self-realization, but rather how he could do the work which his Father had given him to do. From that day in the temple when, at age twelve, he told his parents he must be in his Father's house to the night in Gethsemane when, at the end of his life, he prayed that God's will be done, Jesus devoted himself to the fulfillment of the purpose of God.

Second, Jesus gave himself in ministry to the people about him. It was the servant role he assumed, doing for persons those things which he could offer and which they needed to have done. His main concern was not to expand his own experience or to develop his own self, as though these were adequate goals in themselves. His life was directed toward becoming a person who could be more adequate in a ministry to others.

It is the model of the suffering servant in Isaiah to which the role of Jesus seems to fit most closely.

> He was despised and rejected by men;
>   a man of sorrows, and acquainted with grief. . . .
> Surely he has borne our griefs and carried our sorrows. . . .
> He was wounded for our transgressions,
>   he was bruised for our iniquities;
>   upon him was the chastisement that made us whole,
>   and with his stripes we are healed.
>
> —Isaiah 53:3-5.

The richness of his life came not from what he acquired for himself, not from possessions or knowledge or virtue but from what he was able to offer of himself to those who needed his love.

Jesus is unique. He had a unique relationship with God his Father. He had a distinctive ministry in human history. What, then, does his demonstration of what it means to be human mean for us? Certainly we cannot expect to perform his role, for only he was the full manifestation of God and the full expression of what human life can be.

However, Jesus' life does have meaning for us as we seek to work out for ourselves the purpose we are to fulfill, the humanity we are to realize. Paul put his meaning for us in these terms: "Have this mind among yourselves, which you have in Christ Jesus, who, though he was in the form of God, did not count equality with God a thing to be grasped, but emptied himself, taking the form of a servant, being born in the likeness of men. And being found in human form he humbled himself and became obedient unto death, even death on a cross" (Phil. 2:5-8).

With the mind of Christ within us, we become most fully human not when we are able to exercise our own wills, but when we are responsive to the will of God. With the mind of Christ within us, we glimpse that getting for ourselves is not the purpose for which life is given, whether that getting is possessions or knowledge or heightened consciousness or moral purity. Our lives become most fully human when the gifts we have and the talents we have developed are devoted to bringing a blessing to other persons.

A priority on persons leads us to want for ourselves and for others the fullest possible meaning of humanity. Poverty and oppression can cripple persons, but affluence and freedom do not guarantee that life will be human in the full sense. We are more than creatures of flesh and blood; we are creatures of the spirit. The gospel priority on persons leads us to seek our humanity and the humanity of others as we respond to God and use our lives in ministry. Our spirits are healthy when we know the grace of God and when we can turn outside of ourselves toward others.

Praying for Others

To give priority to persons will lead us to pray for them. As Paul began his letters to the churches, again and again he reminded his readers that he prays for them. To the Romans, for example, he wrote: "For God is my witness, whom I serve with my spirit in the gospel of his Son, that without ceasing I mention you always in my prayers" (Rom. 1:9).

Jesus did not say a great deal about prayer, but the Gospels do show him praying for people. For example, when he talked with Peter about the terrible pressure he would face, Jesus said to him: "Simon, Simon, behold, Satan demanded to have you, that he might sift you like wheat, but I have prayed for you that your faith may not fail; and when you have turned again, strengthen your brethren" (Luke 22:31-32). Repeatedly the biblical witness indicates that when persons care they pray for one another.

When we talk of praying for one another as a way of manifesting a priority on persons, we need to consider both the mystery and the meaning of prayer. Prayer indeed is a mystery; we are just not sure how it "works." There is no way to program prayer, so that certain efforts can be guaranteed to bring specific results. There is really no adequate explanation of how one person praying for another makes any difference to God or to the other person.

Prayer is a mystery also because it probes the profound depths of human existence. There is place for frivolity in life, but prayer is appropriate for more significant concerns. To pray for good weather so a friend can go to the amusement park hardly discerns what prayer is all about. And prayer moves even beyond the "important things" in life. Having enough to eat and finding strength to stand against temptation are indeed important, as Jesus made clear in the prayer which he taught his disciples.

However, prayer for others ranges beyond concern about food, and even beyond beseeching the power to resist temptation. When Jesus saw that Peter's hour of testing and temptation was coming, Jesus prayed for him. Jesus did not pray simply that Peter stand firm and resist temptation. Peter, of course, failed when the test came and denied Jesus three times. But Jesus prayed that "your faith may not fail," and he expressed the urgent hope: "when you have turned again, strengthen your brethren." His prayer was that whatever happened Peter might be led to seek again the way of God, and that his experiences might enable him better to help others. When we pray for others we are led beyond the frivilous and even the important to the most profound possibilities of human existence. There life itself is a mystery, and prayer is a mystery.

To say that prayer is a mystery is not to say that it is meaningless. Nor is it to say that we are totally without understanding. Many things Jesus did not explain about prayer, but one thing he did make clear. Confidence in prayer, whether for ourselves or for others, is based on a conviction about the goodness of God.

Jesus did not present arguments to demonstrate that prayer works. Nor did he point to miraculous occurrences wrought by prayer to justify its practice. Jesus simply prayed, with the obvious conviction that God heard and answered his prayers. He told people to pray with confidence. For "what father among you, if his son asks for a fish, will instead of a fish give him a serpent; or if he asks for an egg, will give him a scorpion? If you then, who are evil, know how to give good gifts to your children, how much more will the heavenly Father give the Holy Spirit to those who ask him? (Luke 11:11-13). We are able to pray for others when we live in the hope of God's love for all his people.

Praying for other persons has meaning, not as a way of persuading God to do something he does not want to do, but as a way of enabling the grace of God to manifest itself in our world. The quality of life is transformed when it is carried on in the midst of a community of people who are praying for one another. We cannot know fully how God will work in the life of a particular person, but we can believe that he uses the network of concern which is created when we reach out in prayer toward others.

There are many ways in which we serve others by giving our money, time, and energy. Prayer is no substitute for these other efforts, but our prayer for others is related to them in two ways. First, when we pray for others we become more ready to be used to bring about the blessing for which we pray. To hold up the need of others before God can make us more sensitive to what we can do to meet that need. Second, there are limits to what one person can do directly for another. There are needs and situations beyond our power to handle, and when we find ourselves facing such circumstances what we can do for another is to pray for him.

Prayer for others is an expression of the importance we put on persons, and it changes significantly the context in which we deal with them. To pray for one who has wronged us helps us to deal creatively with him. To pray for the welfare of a person we are tempted to envy helps us to deal creatively with him. To pray for a person who can be used by us for our own gain helps us to deal creatively with him. An appropriate word for us as we seek to be responsible toward others is this admonition: "Pray at all times in the Spirit, with all prayer and supplication. To that end keep alert with all perseverance, making supplication for all the saints" (Eph. 6:18).

Making Our Witness

Deut. 6:4-9, 20
Matt 28:16-20
Acts 1:6-8

To give priority to persons, as we are concerned for the life of the spirit, will lead us to witness to the faith which sustains our lives. Most of us, at some time, have wished that God would give us a clear demonstration of who he is and what he does—or that he is at all. We would like to know for sure what kind of God there is and what he wants of us. Surely God could give such a convincing demonstration of his existence and his power that we could be absolutely certain about him. But God does not give that kind of infinite knowledge to his creatures. Instead, we live by faith.

However, God does give evidence of himself that enables us to make a meaningful response of faith. There are many ways in which God expresses himself, and in which we have discerned the truth and the power of God. We find evidence of God as we look at the wonder of the world about us. That the world is at all is properly called a miracle. In its beauty, complexity, and order we discern the hand of its Creator.

We find that faith in God is made possible as we reflect on the character of our life on this earth. Deep within us is the conviction that the good, the demand for justice, and the standard of truth are all woven into the fabric of what is most real in our world. The good is not what corrupt and powerful persons say it is; the good is what God has ordained it to be. In our own capacity to transcend ourselves, to look at ourselves and our lives from outside of the confines of this present moment, we are given a hint of the transcendence and the eternity of God.

Faith in God is nurtured for many by an immediate awareness of his presence. The Spirit of God in the midst of our daily life is a vibrant and real experience. A mystical sense of God's presence may be of focused intensity as persons are overwhelmed and seized by God, or it may come as a precious moment of quiet conviction that indeed God is and God cares for us.

For those of us in the Christian community, the Bible gives testimony to the presence and power of God. The biblical account of God's action in the people of Israel has served as convincing demonstration of God's mighty acts in history. The word of the Bible has become the present Word of God addressed to us now, so that in the Scriptures we hear God speak of his love and judgment, his forgiveness and claim. It is to Jesus Christ that the Bible bears witness above all, and it is in Jesus Christ that we find the fullest expression which God has given to us of who he is and what he does.

God has revealed himself in his creation, in history, in the Bible, in mystical experience, and above all in Jesus Christ. But for most of us, awareness of God and his love for us has come initially and persistently through the witness which other persons have made to us. We have seen other people live by faith, and the strength of their lives has made known to us the reality of the God in whom they believed. People have told us about Jesus Christ and interpreted for us the expressions of God in the Bible. Our lives have been sustained by the love of other persons who by their love have made us know what it means for God to love us.

As Jesus hung on the cross, he had remarkably little to show for the labors of his life. There were no buildings standing as a monument to him or as a center for the continuing of his program. There was no book in which Jesus had distilled and written down the wisdom of God. There was no institution ready to continue the functions which Jesus had started. There was not even a list of instructions about what to do next. There were just some people left—frail, discouraged, and dismayed.

But those people were all God needed to continue the ministry of love and truth started by Jesus Christ. While he was still alive, Jesus had sent his disciples and others to minister as they healed, and to witness as they declared that the kingdom of God was near. After his resurrection, Jesus talked to his disciples of what had happened and of what God was doing in all of this. Then he said: "You are my witnesses of these things" (Luke 24:48).

People have helped us to know the love of God. Through the ministry of people our spirits have been strengthened. As we care earnestly and deeply for persons we seek to witness so that they may know the love of God and find their spirits strengthened. We have something to witness to, for we know Jesus Christ. He has given direction, purpose, and meaning to our lives. He has helped us to find a greater nobility. He has given us the assurance of our own worth in God's sight. He has brought to us God's love and the hope of life eternal. We have the rich blessing of God to share with others.

On the day of Pentecost, Peter preached a sermon to the crowd in Jerusalem which moved many people and brought them to faith and repentance. That sermon would hardly "preach" today. If someone stood on a busy corner of the city and spoke the words of Peter, few would stop to listen and fewer still would be persuaded. What Peter said that day is not unimportant or irrelevant for people today. The truth which Peter spoke has to be put into the language, forms, and meanings of today if there is going to be a witness.

There are many ways of witnessing, and it takes thought, sensitivity, and imagination to communicate those things which are most significant to us. There is witness as we speak to each other of what we believe. We need to try to articulate in words our faith so that we can share it. But words are not the only way of witness. A touch of the hand in shared sympathy can speak of the trust in God's care. An act of mercy can testify to the mercy of God. The strength of a person's life can witness to the strength of God in the midst of every circumstance.

Witness is not only by preaching from the pulpit or by handing out pamphlets or by reciting a creed. We seek to become the kind of people in whom the spirit of Christ can dwell that we may be blessed, to be sure; but also in order that in us others may glimpse the great good news of God's love for his people.

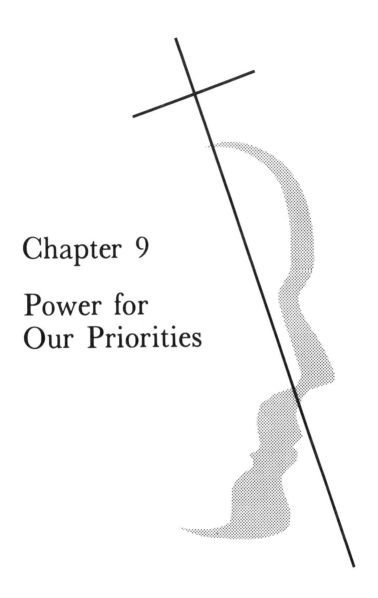

Chapter 9

Power for
Our Priorities

In our discussion together we have explored the thesis that as responsible human beings our first priority is a concern for persons. As we examine our list of priorities in light of the Christian gospel, it bcomes clear that our number one priority is a matter of putting people first. Also, the gospel suggests quite clearly what it means for us to put our priority on persons.

However, the gospel offers us more than merely a mandate to put people first. It is more than a set of standards for moral behavior or a guide for implementing ethical principles in our daily lives. In addition to giving us directives for responsible relationships with one another, the gospel provides us a source of power to enable us to act responsibly—toward God and toward one another.

In this final chapter, we need to consider the manner in which the gospel serves as an enabling power. It is one thing to recognize and accept the stringent demands that the gospel makes upon us. It is something else to comply with these demands. What power does the gospel provide to sustain us as we pursue these lofty ideals?

Power of God's Love

We have affirmed repeatedly that the Christian gospel gives priority to persons. Now let us shift for the moment from talking about persons in general to talking about ourselves. What kind of priority is placed on us—you and me—in this universe? What kind of worth do we have in the total economy of creation? The question of whether our individual lives count for anything very significant haunts us from time to time.

To stand under the stars and ponder what place we have in the vastness of the universe is a humbling moment. We are beginning to glimpse the vastness of space. The earth is a small body in the solar system, and the solar system is a minute part of the ranges of the universe. There are celestial bodies which are millions of light-years removed from us and our planet.

As space reaches beyond our imagination, so also do the dimensions of time. A hundred years, a thousand years seem to us a long time, but all of recorded human history is but a minute fraction in the total span of even the earth's existence. What is the worth of our lives in the context of the dimensions of space and time as we have come to know them?

An awareness of the magnitude of our universe is not the only consideration which raises questions about the worth of one person's life, about the worth of our lives. A threat to meaning is raised when millions of people live together in enormous urban centers. When persons lived in small, stable communities, each had his or her own place and contribution to make. But what does our one life mean in the anonymous mass which is the contemporary city?

Modern warfare raises the issue of what our lives are worth. War is not new in human history, of course, but modern warfare wipes out great numbers of people efficiently, effectively, and impersonally. When people become simply objects to be eliminated or bodies to be counted, what significance do our lives have?

There have been views of the human situation which hold that individual persons are not important. What counts is the long-run achievements of history, or the success of the social system, or the survival of the nation. Meaning for persons is not found in their individual worth but in the contribution which they can make to some larger body or system. If their welfare as persons must be sacrificed for the greater good of the whole, that is a perfectly appropriate sacrifice to demand for they have no worth in themselves.

What are *we* worth? What do our individual, personal, private lives count for? Do our lives really make any difference? The gospel, the good news of the Christian faith, speaks to this anguished question. It is the good news about God's loving care.

There are many ways to talk about God. Aristotle, for example, talked about God as the Unmoved Mover, the source of all that happens. Others have talked about God in terms of a First Principle, the One, the Fullness of Reality, the Object of Ultimate Concern, the Lord of History, and so on. Each of these different ways of talking about God uncover some of the infinite complexity of God and seek to portray the various dimensions which persons have perceived in him.

Talk about God as the Creator, the Infinite Power of Being who is the source of all other beings, helps to keep us from the idolatry of attributing absolute power to any created thing. Talk about God as the Lord of History enables us to affirm that there are significant purposes being worked out in the long travail of persons on this earth.

But the gospel talks about God in more personal terms, about the kind of God who gets involved in our personal needs, our sorrows and struggles. Jesus assures us that God cares for each of us. Granted that the universe is vast in space and time, and that there are billions of people who have lived, are living now, and hopefully will live in the future. But the God Jesus knew, prayed to, and revealed to us is a God big enough to handle all that and still know each one of us.

We recall that Jesus said, "Are not five sparrows sold for two pennies? And not one of them is forgotten before God. Why, even the hairs of your head are all numbered. Fear not; you are of more value than many sparrows" (Luke 12:6-7). Also he told the parable about a man who had a hundred sheep, and if one of them wandered off the shepherd knew it and went to look for it. "So it is not the will of my Father who is in heaven that one of these little ones should perish" (Matt. 18:14).

Each of us at times feel ourselves lost in the vastness of the universe. There are times when we are dealt with as one of the mass. We struggle to prove to ourselves that we really are worth something because we are needed by someone, or because we have an important job, or because we have the right connections. All of that is very human, for to be needed, to have a good job, and to have good connections do give us a sense of our worth in a hostile and threatening world.

But the good news of Jesus is that God cares for us, that God knows about us, and that God loves us. We do not have to do anything to be worth something. We do not have to earn our significance. We do not have to beat out other people to prove that we are important. We are worth something, everything, because we are known and cared for by God whom Jesus taught us to call our Father. We have significance in this great big, mysterious universe because God thinks that we are important.

Knowing God's love for us, as it has been so dramatically expressed in Jesus Christ, gives power which enables us to give priority to persons. Stated in the broadest term, we are able to love and care for others because we have been loved and cared for by God. Gordon Kaufman described the enabling power of the gospel as follows:

> This new awareness of the presence of God's love in their midst freed the first Christians of their doubts and fears. No longer had man to live a self-centered existence, always building walls between himself and others for protection

against betrayals and hurts, for it was now clear that God—the very foundation of all existence—is absolutely trustworthy; he never betrays. So man, also, could take the risk of loving God and his fellows without reservation. Thus God's act of love, in making it possible for man to love, literally transformed him into a 'new creation' (2 Cor. 5:17) no longer centered in himself but centered instead in God"[1]

In the words of the author of First John: "We love, because he first loved us" (4:14). It is God's love for us which gives us the assurance of our worth, so that we can affirm the worth of others in love. We can love when we have been loved, and God's wondrous love has been made known to us in Jesus Christ.

The priority which we would give to persons is made possible by the enabling power of God in many ways. We have talked of loyalty as one expression of our priority on persons. We are able to be loyal because we believe that God is loyal to us. We are able to be loyal to others because God's love for us gives us the security which enables us to risk ourselves for others. Our lives have been transformed and enriched by the impact of God's commitment to us, a commitment which led him to the giving of himself in Jesus Christ. Such a commitment to us makes possible our commitment to others.

God's love enables us to be sensitive to others and to express a priority on persons in meaningful ways. When we no longer have to be so concerned about our own worth, we are freed to pay some attention to others. The humility which enables us to be open to others becomes possible as Jesus Christ ministers to us. In the presence of the Lord, arrogance and pride and self-seeking are seen to be empty and hollow. God's assurance of our worth makes possible our humility, for it is those who know their worth before God who can be meek and humble.

To be genuinely concerned about others demands extraordinary persistence, for people can be difficult and trying. How can we go on caring when we are rebuffed, when we are tired, when we are discouraged? In part we can persist because God has persisted with us.

---

[1]Gordon Kaufman, *The Context of Decision.* Abingdon Press, 1961, p. 43.

Through one of the Old Testament prophets, God speaks of how he has loved his people Israel since they were children. Event though his people turned from him to worship idols, God says that he cannot give them up. He cries out:

> How can I give you up, O Ephraim!
> How can I hand you over, O Israel!
> My heart recoils within me,
>   my compassion grows warm and tender . . .
> for I am God and not man,
>   the Holy One in your midst,
>   and I will not come to destroy.
>
> —Hosea 11:8-9

Finally God sent Jesus Christ to bring his love and care into the world. God has persisted with us, as he did with Israel, when we have rebelled against him. He has sustained us in his love beyond all that we deserve. We can persist in our care for others because God has persisted in his care for us.

Persistence in caring for other persons means forgiving them when they have wronged us. How difficult it is to forgive someone who has hurt us deeply. Vengeance comes easy for us; hate flows readily through our minds and spirits, we could care less what happens to the person who has done damage to us. Reactions like these fill our minds until we experience in our own lives the forgiveness of God. Then it becomes possible that even we may forgive out of love and compassion for those who have done the wrong.

How different our lives might have been if we had not received the awesome love of God, the love made known to his people Israel, the love revealed in its fullness in Jesus Christ. Because we do know that love, there is within us the potential for really caring about people. Because we are cared for, we can care. Because we know our worth before God, we can give worth to others.

God's Triumphant Power

It is often discouraging to try to put persons first. How difficult it is to make life human, in any definition of humanity. How strong are the forces of destruction and dehumanization. How frail are our own commitments and capacities. If we set out to build a better world by our own efforts alone, how overwhelming the task.

But the final word in our reflection on how we are to live responsibly with others, and what it means to put persons first, is not about the difficulties or our weaknesses. It is about the power of God manifest in Jesus Christ and above all in his resurrection. Easter is the major festival of the Christian year. Sunday is the holy day in the Christian tradition. Easter and Sunday both celebrate the raising of Jesus Christ from the dead. When Paul wrote to the Corinthians about the basic teachings of the Christian faith, he declared: "I delivered to you as of first importance what I also received, that Christ died for our sins in accordance with the scriptures, that he was buried, that he was raised on the third day in accordance with the scriptures" (1 Cor. 15:3-4).

For the Christian faith, the teaching of Jesus is important. The quality of the life of Jesus is significant. But at the center of the faith is the affirmation of the resurrection of Jesus. What manner of happening is this? We can know what happened on Good Friday as Jesus was nailed to the cross. But what happened on Easter Sunday when Jesus was raised from the dead? A person executed is something we can fit into our normal framework of experience. A person appearing from the dead does not fit into the regular ordering of our world.

The resurrection of Jesus, some may argue, can be dismissed as an illusion or a clever fabrication. Such a quick dismissal hardly does justice to the power which has been generated in our world by the Christian faith. It does need to be said that there is no way the resurrection of Jesus can be "proved" by any of the normal means of proof in human history or experience. But to say that the resurrection cannot be proved does not mean that it must be dismissed as sheer nonsense.

Conviction about the resurrection grows in faith. We have evidence to nurture that faith. There is the testimony of Paul who stated that the risen Christ had appeared to Cephas, to the twelve, to more than five hundred persons at one time, to James, and "last of all . . . he appeared also to me" (1 Cor. 15:8). Moreover, there is the fact of the radical transformation of Jesus' immediate disciples, changing them from frightened, defeated men to courageous leaders. There is also the continuing reality of the church which has witnessed to the abiding presence of Christ in its life across the centuries.

The fundamental conviction of the faith, however, is that *God's* power and love were manifest in the resurrection of Jesus Christ. If the resurrection is to be believed, it is because of who God is. What exactly happened on that first day of the week after the crucifixion is shrouded in some mystery. The gospel accounts differ in detail, for they were written some time after the events and reflect the different perspectives of different people. We are involved here in a happening beyond the ordinary course of human events. But these accounts communicate the overwhelming conviction that Jesus, who had been Master and Teacher to his disciples, was once again present in their midst.

The question needs to be asked: Why the resurrection of Jesus? For what purpose did God act to raise him from the dead? Was it a dramatic miracle designed to impress the world? Was it a spectacular display of power to prove that God could do it if he wanted to? Was it a triumphant event pulled off to confound the enemies of God? For what purpose did God raise Jesus?

A look at the Gospel accounts gives some clue to the answers to these questions:

Jesus appeared to two men on the road to Emmaus. They were leaving Jerusalem where their hopes had been shattered by the death of Jesus. As Jesus approached them they were close to despair. They told him of the tragic events in Jerusalem, and then Jesus interpreted for them the scriptures of their people. When they stopped for the evening, Jesus broke bread with them, and suddenly they knew him. Then they remembered: "Did not our hearts burn within us while he talked to us on the road, while he opened to us the scriptures?" (Luke 24:32). And they raced back to Jerusalem to tell the disciples.

Jesus encountered Mary as she stood weeping outside the tomb. Her eyes filled with tears, Mary did not recognize him; she thought that he was the gardener. Then Jesus spoke her name and she knew him. Suddenly her sorrow turned to overwhelming joy, and she hastened from the tomb to cry to the disciples, "I have seen the Lord" (John 20:18).

Jesus appeared to most of his disciples as they were gathered on the evening of that first day of the week. The doors were shut tight because they were fearful of what might happen to them.

After all, Jesus had been crucified and the persecution might well continue. Suddenly Jesus was there and "the disciples were glad when they saw the Lord. Jesus said to them again, 'Peace be with you. As the Father has sent me, even so I send you.' And when he had said this, he breathed on them, and said to them, 'Receive the Holy Spirit' " (John 20:20-22).

One of the disciples was absent from that gathering, and Jesus returned later to deal with the doubts of Thomas. Once again Jesus bestowed his peace upon his followers and then he offered Thomas the proof which Thomas had demanded, to see his hands and put his finger in the nail marks and his hand in his side. Confronted by Jesus who called him not to be faithless but believing, Thomas cried out, "My Lord and my God" (John 20:28).

For what purpose was the resurrection of Jesus? Repeatedly, after his resurrection, Jesus came to his people and ministered to them. When they were sorrowful, he brought them joy. When they were in despair, he brought them comfort. When they were afraid, he brought them his peace. When they were unbelieving, he brought them to faith. The resurrection of Jesus is another expression of the profound concern of God for his people. When Jesus was raised from the dead he did not make a spectacular demonstration in the middle of the city. He quietly went to the people who wept and feared, and he ministered to them.

The resurrection of Jesus is testimony to us of the triumph of life over death. Death of the body is the hard, brutal reality which every person faces. This fact cannot be denied or ignored as we talk about putting priority on persons. Death of the spirit makes hollow the existence of many. God brings the assurance that death is not the final word as Jesus Christ, raised from the dead, enters into relationship with his people.

The resurrection of Jesus is assurance to us of the staying power of the good in the face of the awesome power of evil. In his life Jesus embodied goodness, the purity and holiness of God. But the good man was destroyed and the powers of evil seemed triumphant, as they have so often in the struggles of persons on this earth. But evil did not have the last word, and Jesus came to his people as witness to them that his goodness endures.

The resurrection of Jesus is witness to us of the awesome capacity of love. Hatred, bitterness, abuse permeated the events of Good Friday as Jesus was scourged, mocked, spit upon, and finally killed. But Jesus went on loving that day, and he came again in love to his people on the third day.

The presence of the risen Christ with us shapes our relationships with others and offers the power to live with them in Christian concern. There is corruption in every human relationship. People try to use one another in blatant or subtle ways. People become impatient and hurt one another. People refuse to accept their responsibility to one another and deny one another, even as the disciples denied they had ever known Jesus. But Jesus' restoration of his relationship with his disciples affirm that we can reach out toward others, and that goodness and love may yet triumph over all that pushes us away from people.

The resurrection affirms the eternal quality of human life and relationships. Our relationships with others are serious, not necessarily solemn, but serious. Dealing with others is not a frivolous matter of the moment to be lightly forgotten. By his resurrection, Jesus demonstrated that even death could not break the bond which bound him to those he loved. We deal with eternal things, things of vast significance, when we create ties with other persons.

Finally, the resurrection witnesses anew to the power which is unleashed in persons through their relationships. The death of Jesus brought those who had known him to the most desolate, despairing, frightening moment of their lives. Their world was shattered. But by being with them once again, Jesus restored their lives.

It is the living Lord's relationship with us which heals our hurt and calms our fear. And that healing can come also through us to others. We enter into relationship with others in the hope that the life, the good, and the love brought anew into the world by the resurrection of Jesus Christ will flow through us to others and through others to us.